Twayne's English Authors Series

Sylvia E. Bowman, *Editor*

INDIANA UNIVERSITY

Norman Nicholson

TEAS 153

NORMAN NICHOLSON

By PHILIP GARDNER

Memorial University of Newfoundland

Twayne Publishers, Inc.   ::   New York

PR
6027
.I295
Z7

ISBN 0-8057-1418-9

66929

To George Rylands

Preface

Although Norman Nicholson has never been a fashionable writer, he has created during the past twenty-five years or so a body of poetry whose close combination of Christian belief and regional subject matter can reasonably be described as unique in contemporary British literature. In addition, his four verse plays have been performed often enough to suggest that they have a strong appeal for the type of audiences and acting groups at which they were aimed.

Nicholson's poetry and plays are still, however, far from being as widely known as they deserve to be. Far too many people, on hearing Nicholson's name, cannot place it, or know him only through one particular book — usually one which is not central to his significant creative achievement. They may know him as, for instance, the editor of the *Penguin Anthology of Religious Verse,* as the author of the guidebook *Cumberland and Westmorland,* or as the sympathetic and sensitive critic of *William Cowper;* but they are quite likely not to know at all that he is a poet. Those who are aware that he is a poet and versedramatist are often aware only in a fragmentary way, having read *Five Rivers* or *The Old Man of the Mountains* but nothing else.

Nor has Nicholson been well served by critics, despite the serious and often very complimentary reviews accorded his volumes when they first appeared. No more than a handful of short articles have been written about his poetry, and one or two of his verse plays have been briefly surveyed in a few books dealing with modern Christian verse drama, but no full-length study of his work has so far been published.

My concentration in this book is on Nicholson's poetry and plays, both as works of imagination and craftsmanship and as presentations of a Christian view of life solidly rooted in the experiences and places of one particular area. These twin concerns — which may be summarized as region and religion — also provide the impetus for Nicholson's wide range of other works, which include topographical books together with many articles and broadcast talks. Insofar as these peripheral works usefully illuminate my main topic, I shall make reference to them; but, because they are discursive and descriptive rather than creative, I shall not examine them for their own sake. Considerations of space have precluded a section on Nicholson's critical books and on his two interesting but minor novels, *The Fire of the Lord* and *The Green Shore*. The novels, however, are discussed in a recent article by this writer listed in the Bibliography.

Since Nicholson's creative work is unfamiliar to a large number of readers, knowledge of his life and of the part of England in which that life has been entirely led cannot be assumed. My first chapter is, therefore, devoted to providing a context of biography and geography which will enable Nicholson's poetry and plays to be more fully understood and appreciated. Chapter 2 is concerned with Nicholson's apprentice work in poetry, from 1937 to 1943, when he was strongly influenced by T. S. Eliot and the social poets of the 1930s.

Chapter 3 deals with Nicholson's three main volumes of poetry, *Five Rivers, Rock Face,* and *The Pot Geranium.* Chapter 4 surveys Nicholson's more recent poetry: after a long fallow period starting about 1958, Nicholson recovered his poetic impetus in 1965 and has moved in directions exciting and in some ways quite new. Chapter 5 describes the aims and evaluates the success of his four verse plays, written between 1944 and 1959, and links them with the revival of Christian verse drama to which they generically belong.

Nicholson's activity, certainly as a poet, is obviously by no means exhausted, but I attempt in Chapter 6 to survey his varying critical reputation and to reach some tentative conclusions about his position in the British literary scene—both generally and as a unique contributor to the "regional" tradition. Paradoxically, his contribution to this tradition gives him his special claim to notice and yet, perhaps, explains the critical neglect of his work.

One final word should be said. I have read and reread Nicholson's poetry and verse plays with the keenest pleasure over the past fifteen years. My hope is that the following pages may communicate something of this pleasure and, by doing so, enlarge to some degree the audience for Nicholson's work. If my pages betray their subject, I hope that the reader will ignore them and turn nevertheless to Nicholson's own. There, at any rate, he will not be disappointed.

Memorial University of Newfoundland

PHILIP GARDNER

Acknowledgments

To prepare a book on a living writer is to accumulate a particularly personal kind of indebtedness. I take great pleasure in acknowledging it here.

My greatest debt is to Norman Nicholson himself. Over a number of years he has welcomed me into his home, answered my many questions, and given me access to much material not otherwise easily come by. I am also grateful to his wife, Mrs. Yvonne Nicholson, and to his stepmother, Mrs. Rosetta Nicholson (who died in 1969), for putting themselves out to make my visits to Millom even more enjoyable.

My documentation of Nicholson's early life and poetic development would hardly have been possible but for the generous assistance of Brother George Every, S.S.M., and Mrs. C. B. Schiff (née Satterthwaite), who allowed me to consult many letters and manuscripts of poems, in addition to giving freely of their time and memories. For my introduction to Mrs. Schiff, I am indebted to Professor W. Moelwyn Merchant of Exeter University. Mrs. Anne Ridler discussed Nicholson's work with me and sent me a copy of a letter to her on that subject from T. S. Eliot. Miss Pamela Keily gave me information about her productions of *Birth by Drowning;* and Professor William Brasmer, of Denison University, Ohio, sent me many details of his university's productions of *A Match for the Devil* and *Prophesy to the Wind.* Miss H. Q. Iredale, of St. Katharine's College, Liverpool, lent me useful material on the history of Millom.

I am grateful to The Canada Council, whose award of a Doctoral Fellowship enabled me to pursue for two years the research which contributed to the writing of this book, and to the Memorial University of Newfoundland for granting me the necessary leave of absence. In a different and very much longer form my work on Norman Nicholson earned me the degree of Doctor in Philosophy at the University of Liverpool, and I should like to take this opportunity to thank Professor Kenneth Muir and my supervisor, the late Professor Kenneth Allott, for the unstinting help they gave me during my time there. I am also indebted to Professor Sylvia Bowman for a number of editorial improvements to the text of this book.

I am grateful to Faber and Faber Ltd. for permission to quote material from *Five Rivers* and *The Old Man of the Mountains;* and to Faber and Faber Ltd., Norman Nicholson, and David Higham Associates Ltd. for permission to quote material from *The Pot Geranium.*

My final debt is to my wife and colleague, Averil Gardner, who has always been willing to discuss Nicholson's work with me and to assist me in improving my own.

Contents

Chronology

1914   Norman Nicholson born at 14 St. George's Terrace, Millom, Cumberland.
1919   Mother died.
1922   Father remarried.
1925   Nicholson entered Millom Secondary School.
1929   Confirmed into Church of England.
1930   Discovered to have tuberculosis. Formal education ceased.
1930-
1932   In sanatorium at Linford, near Ringwood, Hampshire.
1932-
1934   Returned to Millom. Alienated from local environment and formal religion.
1934   First read poetry of T. S. Eliot. Beginning of gradual re-acceptance of local environment.
c. 1935 Beginning of friendship with the Reverend (later Canon) Samuel Taylor, Vicar of Holy Trinity, Millom.
1937   Nicholson's earliest poems first read by Brother George Every, a contributor to *The Criterion* and a friend of T. S. Eliot. Beginning of long correspondence and friendship between Nicholson and Every.
1938   First important publication of Nicholson's work in *Poetry* (Chicago). First meeting, in London, with T. S. Eliot.
1938-
1943   Lectured for Workers' Educational Association in Millom, Whitehaven, and St. Bees.
1939   Lectured at Student Christian Movement conference at Swanwick, Derbyshire.
1940   Returned to full communicant membership of Church of England.
1942   Edited *Anthology of Religious Verse* for Penguin Books.

1943   *Man and Literature* published. *Selected Poems* (with J. C. Hall and Keith Douglas).

1944   *Five Rivers. The Fire of the Lord.*

1945   Awarded Heinemann Prize for *Five Rivers*. Fellow of the Royal Society of Literature. *The Old Man of the Mountains* first performed in London.

1946   *The Old Man of the Mountains* published.

1947   *The Green Shore.*

1948   *Rock Face.*

1949   *Cumberland and Westmorland.* First performance of *Prophesy to the Wind.*

1950   *Prophesy to the Wind* published. *H. G. Wells.*

1951   Approached by The British Council to go to India on a lecture tour. Obliged to decline because of poor health. *William Cowper.*

1953   *A Match for the Devil* performed at Edinburgh Festival.

1954   *The Pot Geranium.* Father died. Nicholson managed family shop for two months.

1955   *A Match for the Devil* published. *The Lakers.*

1956   Married Yvonne Edith Gardner, a schoolteacher who came to Millom from London.

1959   First performance of *Birth by Drowning.* Awarded honorary degree of Master of Arts by Manchester University.

1960   *Birth by Drowning* published.

1965   Informed that all traces of tuberculosis had disappeared.

1967   *No Star on the Way Back.* Awarded Cholmondeley Prize for Poetry (shared with Seamus Heaney and Brian Jones).

1969   Death of Nicholson's stepmother. Awarded £500 grant by Northern Arts Association. *Greater Lakeland* published.

1970   Gave Memorial Lecture at Cockermouth, Cumberland, on the occasion of the Bicentenary of birth of William Wordsworth.

1972   Fourth volume of poetry. *A Local Habitation*, published by Faber and Faber Ltd.

CHAPTER 1

Landscape and Life

I N August, 1967, three poets divided between them the recently established Cholmondeley Prize for Poetry. Two were young poets just beginning to make a name for themselves—Seamus Heaney and Brian Jones. The third was Norman Nicholson, who at the age of fifty-three had published three important volumes and had thirty years of experience as a poet behind him. When he was thirty Nicholson had won the Heinemann Prize for Poetry with his first volume, *Five Rivers.* That he should also have won another award, so much later and in such youthful company, points to the continued vitality and relevance of his work.

In making the presentation, William Plomer, one of the judges, referred to Nicholson as a "regional" poet. By this he meant to indicate simply that Nicholson is thought of as a Cumbrian poet, as the product and as the spokesman of a particular area. He emphatically did not mean to imply that Nicholson is a regional writer in any restricted sense—as one whose work is outside and irrelevant to the dominant metropolitan literary tradition. The very fact that the award was made by a panel of judges consisting of such well-known, non-regional writers as L. P. Hartley, Plomer himself, and Alan Ross, editor of the influential *London Magazine,* suggests strongly that Nicholson's poetry is not limited in its appeal and that its regional material serves a view of life which is widely understandable. The Cholmondeley Prize was given, not to a "special case," but simply to a good poet.

Nevertheless, it is in terms of regionalism that Nicholson's kind of poetry may most conveniently be seen. As a literary category, regionalism has been defined as "the tendency of some writers to set their works in a particular locality, presented in some detail, as affecting the lives and fortunes of the inhabitants."[1] This definition, intended to characterize the regional novelist, needs little adaptation to apply to the regional poet. He himself, if no one else, is an "inhabitant"

[15]

of his poems; and the region is important in that it affects his life and conditions his subject matter and his response to it. Phyllis Bentley, in her study *The English Regional Novel,*[2] points out another trademark of the "regional" writer—his interest in the ordinary, the day-to-day.

All these characteristics of regionalism are present in Nicholson's poetry, and he himself would be the first to protest if its regional element were underplayed. Its universality is, for him, gained not merely from a regional starting point, but because of that starting-point; and he feels a certain resentment against critics who are unnecessarily determined to "rescue" a writer like Hardy, for instance, from what is to them the pejorative label of "regionalist": "To refuse to call a poet 'regional' when he so obviously is, is to fail to understand part of what he is saying: to insist on the 'universal' aspect of his work at the expense of the local is to show that we have missed something of that which makes him universal."[3]

For Nicholson, a writer's local roots are very important. He himself has proved quite willing, in a number of broadcast talks, to defend their value and to face any criticism that may inhere in the "regional" label by describing himself, more polemically, as a "provincial." In challenging the stock response to this word (which for Dr. Johnson was synonymous with "rude and unpolished," and which even for the *New English Dictionary* implies a narrowness of outlook), Nicholson has sought to show that the man from "the provinces" (and, by extension, the provincial writer) is more closely in touch than his metropolitan cousin with truths fundamental to human life: the relationship between man and his environment, and, ultimately, between man and God. Since Nicholson's region is, therefore, so fundamental to his poetry, providing both its setting and the soil from which its universal themes grow, we must consider his region and his early life and development in it before examining the poems and verse plays themselves.

I   The Poet's Landscape

Except for a period of two years when in his teens, Norman Nicholson has spent the whole of his life in the small, South Cumberland town of Millom, whose existence for a hundred years has been centered round the mining of iron ore and the making of steel. The places mentioned or described in Nicholson's poetry are remote from the itineraries of the ordinary tourist who visits the Lake District

[16]

sections of Cumberland and Westmorland in search of William Wordsworth or mountain climbing. The Nicholson country, the area of which as a poet he is the "sole proprietor" (to use William Faulkner's term[4]), is mainly West Cumberland and South Cumberland, a strip of comparatively narrow coastal land running some forty miles from the port of Whitehaven in the north to where Millom juts into the Duddon estuary.

An out-of-the-way area, well to one side of the main railway routes and cut off from easy access by road by the western edge of the Lake District mountain dome, the region is also one of considerable beauty. It has not only the elemental natural beauty of sea cliffs, green turf edging its little-frequented shore, varicolored mountain slopes rising inland and at one point, near the village of Bootle, looming heavily just above the coastal road, but also the beauty produced by the long human associations of the landscape. The area is, in effect, a palimpsest of history, a microcosm of human evolution and development. Beneath everything is the stratified, prehistorical rock itself, which towers eastwards as Great Gable and Bowfell and which thrusts into the Irish Sea as the sandstone of St. Bees Head. Behind Whitehaven, lie the coal measures, and under Millom, the iron-ore veins, which have determined the region's modern economy. At Swinside, the megalith builders of over a thousand years before Christ raised one of their stone circles, and at Ravenglass are the remains of a Roman bath house. In the small churchyard at Gosforth stands one of the most famous Norse crosses in England. The whole area abounds in Norse place names, and the very words used (often in Nicholson's poems) to describe features of the landscape are of Norse origin: *fell, scree, tarn, beck, pike, force, thwaite*; and Nicholson's own middle name is Cornthwaite. Egremont's sandstone castle was part of Cumberland's defenses against the Border raids of the Middle Ages, and the contemporary world is most obviously present in the experimental weapons establishment at Eskmeals and, farther up the coast, at Sellafield where the cooling towers of the Calder Hall atomic factory bulge whitely upwards and darken the air with their immense oozings of smoke. Almost all these features of the West Cumberland landscape have somewhere or other their place in Nicholson's poetry.

Millom itself is situated at the southern end of the region, and is more than one of its most important focal points, to which the roads from outlying hamlets and farms converge. The town acts as the hub of

[17]

Nicholson's poetic imagination:[5] its church spire is visible for miles up the Irish Sea coast, its ironworks dominate the Duddon estuary "like a huge battle-ship sailing out with all funnels smoking,"[6] and the whalebacked mountain of Black Combe rises just to the north of the town. Millom is to Nicholson what Oxford, Mississippi, is to William Faulkner, what the Five Towns are to Arnold Bennett and what Manosque is to the French novelist Jean Giono. This place Nicholson has wished to present in all its local individuality, but also as a microcosm of the world as a whole, for it displays within convenient limits all those aspects of human life which are to him of most importance.

Millom is not, however, a prepossessing place. Despite its fine sandstone church and the quaintness of its market clock, set in a pewter dome resembling an English policeman's helmet, its architecture is rather drab, and the oblong slagbank which bulks behind its houses fails to provoke the same instant excitement as a mountain would. But Millom's very ordinariness is a kind of asset; in not being distracted by the outward appearance of a beautiful spot, the visitor is forced to look beneath the surface for what Nicholson once called

> ... the truth beneath it all:
> Beneath the shape, the wall, beneath the wall, the stone,
> Beneath the stone, the idea of a stone,
> Beneath the idea, the love.[7]

Nicholson's poetry brings Millom fully alive in imaginative terms, but basic to his imagination is a respect for facts and an ability to use these to discover a fundamental unity beneath the apparent discreteness of visual phenomena—a mountain, a slagbank, an ironworks and the houses which surround it. This unity comprises the beginning and end of a process to which man, as miner and as foundry worker, is central. The light that transforms the drabness of Millom in Nicholson's best poetry is not a glitter of words, not the diamanté of a sparkling vocabulary: it is the intense inward glow of the actual, that has been perceived and transmitted by one who knows his subject matter through years of firsthand experience and is fully aware of "a human meaning to the scene."[8]

A very few of the most significant items in Millom's history may enable the reader to share something of the life out of which Nicholson's poetry springs. The town as it exists today and with which Nicholson is essentially concerned is almost entirely the creation of the

Victorian Age—a creation based on the discovery in 1860 of large deposits of hematite iron ore near Hodbarrow Point a mile or so south of Millom. The decade which followed this discovery has been referred to by Nicholson as the "Iron Rush."[9] An area whose scanty population consisted in 1861 of Cumbrians and North Lancastrians saw the influx , from 1865, of a stream of "off-comers": Englishmen from other northern counties, Irishmen, and former tin miners from Devon and Cornwall. Among these immigrants were Norman Nicholson's paternal grandparents and the Devonian forebears of his stepmother-to-be. The population doubled almost overnight, and by 1866 the iron mines were producing three thousand tons of ore a week. In September, 1867, the newly constructed Millom ironworks began operation and continued its activity for just over a hundred years. By 1867, plans for a new town of Millom, intended to be "a sort of model town,"[10] were being put into effect; and in 1874 the most crowded parts of Millom held between three and four thousand people.

Along with the final shaping of the town into its present form were the years of its greatest prosperity, from 1870 to the turn of the century. After 1880, the annual output of the mines, famous throughout England for the size and high quality of their yield, was nearly 350,000 tons; and in 1891, their peak year, they produced 535,000 tons of ore. The discovery of iron left its mark not only in the virtual creation of Millom, but in other changes it brought to the landscape: firstly, the gradual building of the slagbank which is now so prominent a feature in the town; second, the considerable alteration (described in 1966 in Nicholson's poem "Bee Orchid at Hodbarrow") which mining brought to the shape of the coastline to the south.

Millom today is a quiet town compared to what it was in those boom years. The depression of the 1920s and 1930s affected it, as it did all the industrial areas of the West Cumberland coast; and its population today is only about seven thousand. Yet well into this century one mine continued to produce hematite ore, and in a recent poem called "The Borehole" Nicholson recalls a period in his youth when ore prospecting was still going on. Until 1968, when Millom Ironworks was suddenly closed by a government decision whose adverse local effects have still to be surmounted, iron, imported from abroad, was smelted into steel of extremely high quality.

When something of Millom's history is known, it can be seen that there is more to the town than the appearance it presents to a visitor—a

[19]

small hotel, a workingmen's club, a couple of banks, the market hall with its quaint clock, the steepled Victorian church, all clustered around a quiet square in which the arrival and departure of a bus is an event. The past is not difficult to discern: the street that appears on plans of the town but was never actually built,[11] the farm which still juts out "like a crag" from the houses "shunted firm against;"[12] when the town grew up, the gridiron pattern of the new town, the small quarry in Holborn Hill out of which came "hard on five hundred houses" of that new town.[13] A walk out of Millom towards Hodbarrow Point is a tour into the past, into an Audenesque landscape of abandoned mine workings and rusty railway lines overgrown with brambles. Beyond the old, deserted lighthouse is the grass-choked shaft of Towsey Hole where the first deposit of hematite was found, and on the right, across a subsidence crater like the bowl of an extinct volcano, the Inner Barrier, "collapsed like the Great Wall of China. . .tumbles into the sand now, its central piers already engulfed."[14]

Given such a landscape, one where industry and its natural origins are visible simultaneously, it is easy to see how Nicholson could describe Millom as ". . . a town which has sprung out of the land almost as naturally as weeds spring up when a wood is felled or burned down: the ore out of the rock; the iron out of the ore; and the houses, the streets, the churches, the schools, very nearly the children themselves, out of the iron."[15]

As well as producing in a sensitive observer the feeling that the place originates from an almost completely natural process, a town like Millom, centered on one industry, can also create in its small population the feeling that it belongs to a shared environment, can create for any one person—the writer, for instance—the feeling that his life is interwoven with that of his fellows: "Here is a continual approach and meeting, an interpatterning and overlapping of individual lives, a counterpointing of one man's day with that of another."[16] And when a place is as young as Millom, when its entire growth as an industrial town can virtually be recapitulated in living memory, this "counterpointing" in the present is underpinned by a sense of continuity with the past, one based on a network of common experiences and memories:

These people have been fed and watered by the same sun and wind and weather. They have all felt the same excitement queueing for the children's matinee outside the same cinema; they have all run over the railway bridge, hearts backfiring like motor-bikes, fearing they would miss the same train. They have known the tension that comes upon a community at a time of local anxieties: the day the tide broke through the sea-wall; the day the viaduct was found unsafe: the week when the roads and railways were blocked and not a soul could enter or leave the town for six days.[17]

The two ideas demonstrated by these three prose quotations—the connection of man with nature, and of man with man in past and present dimensions—are central to a proper understanding of Norman Nicholson's poetry. Life in Millom has brought such ideas forcefully to his notice; and, had he left it, or had he belonged to some other kind of town—perhaps a larger one—it is doubtful whether his poetry would have developed the way it has. It is necessary, however, to see the poet growing up in the landscape which his poetry has been concerned to describe and interpret, not only for those with whom he shared it but also for an outside audience which he feels to be, basically, not so very different from them.

II *Nicholson's Early Life*

Nicholson's background is solidly North Country working- and lower-middle-class; his family has been rooted in Millom for three generations, and its history is in effect the history of the town itself. His paternal grandfather originally farmed near Cartmel in North Lancashire; but, soon after marrying, he brought his wife to Millom in 1867. There he worked for the newly-established ironworks, and he was among the pioneers who shared in the making of the Victorian industrial town. Richard Nicholson and his wife had fourteen sons, of whom Joseph, the poet's father, was born in 1877, the year in which the new steepled sandstone parish church of St. George began to rise opposite the market square. After many years spent in apprenticeship to a local tailor, Joseph Nicholson established his own tailoring business in a shop just opposite the market square. He married Edith Cornthwaite, the daughter of a Millom butcher; and over his shop at 14 St. George's Terrace their only child, Norman Cornthwaite Nicholson, was born on January 8, 1914. In this same three-storied terraced house, Nicholson has spent his entire life.

In 1919 Nicholson's mother died, one of the many victims of the

[21]

worldwide epidemic of "Spanish" influenza; and in 1922 Joseph Nicholson married again. His second wife, Rosetta Sobey, who managed a piano shop a few doors away, had equally deep roots in Millom: she came of a family of Devon tin miners who had emigrated to the nearby village of Haverigg in the 1870s. Nicholson's stepmother was a Methodist, and he soon found himself attending the local Wesleyan chapel and Sunday school. Thus, though his Anglican father had had him baptized in St. George's Church, it was in a Methodist atmosphere that his childhood was mostly spent.[18] Methodism was so closely linked—by means of concerts, socials, bazaars, and "Faith Teas"—with the communal life of the town that Nicholson was more aware of its social than of its religious elements. Yet there is little doubt that the oratory of Methodist local preachers and the hymns of John Wesley and Isaac Watts had a strong effect on his boyhood imagination. Nicholson later said that, "although I have now found my home in the Anglican church, I feel that as a poet I draw more strength from my experiences of Methodism."[19]

After a primary education at the local boys' school, Nicholson won a scholarship to Millom Secondary (Grammar) School in 1925. His entrance results were the highest in the county, he was regularly at the head of his class, and by 1929 it was quite clear that he was destined for some kind of academic career. In exploring the countryside round Millom, he began to feel that his home town was "small, old-fashioned, and tagged to the fraying end of what seemed to be a worn-out social era." His ambitions were those predictable in any clever boy living in a small provincial town: ". . .like most of us at that time at the local grammar school, I saw no future in the town—or not, at any rate, for me. I saw myself as going to the university, getting a degree, becoming a teacher and escaping into the wide world."[20]

These ambitions led him back to the Church of England in which he had been baptized. He was confirmed in 1929, mainly for the practical reason that, according to local myth, "you had a better chance of entering a college if you had been confirmed."[21] But despite the practical motive behind his confirmation, it did have the result of bringing religion to his consciousness in a personal way: "I knelt for long periods in my bedroom, praying and 'preparing' myself for the next Sunday's communion. The thought of the moment of consecration could make me shake like a fever."[22] The reaction to this typically adolescent devotion—"sixteen year old materialism and complete lack of interest in religion"[23] — was not long in coming; but Nicholson's intense initial response to his confirmation may be said to have laid half the foundation for his later poetry—its deeply Christian attitude. The other half of the foundation—his poetry's concern with regional experience—was laid, in effect, the following year. In 1930 Nicholson's ambition of "escaping into the wide world" by going to a university was frustrated by the discovery that he had contracted tuberculosis. Shattering though this discovery must have been to him at the time, it may be claimed in retrospect that tuberculosis was the single most important factor in Nicholson's life—and not, in the long run, a negative factor. It determined his life's development, forced him to stand still and take stock, and made him into the kind of poet he is; for his illness forced him to stay at home rather than become one of the many "strangers in a hundred other places" whom the local Grammar School "creams off. . . and rarely. . . calls back."[24] Hindsight has certainly enabled Nicholson himself to see his illness as almost an act of fate, or even as divine intervention. Describing his gradual approach to Christianity, he said many years later that "at this point the course of my life was signalled on to a new track."[25] He also said, elsewhere, that he would have left Millom "but for the grace of God and the tubercle bacillus."[26]

The immediate effect of the discovery was to end Nicholson's formal education. In the autumn of 1930 he was sent to a private sanatorium at Linford on the extreme western edge of the New Forest in Hampshire—a landscape very different from that in which he had grown up, and one which "still belonged to the age of Edwardian cyclists, naturalists and Georgian poets."[27] Here he spent fifteen months in bed, and the experience of isolated closeness to nature was for him the equivalent of a university education:

As season followed season, I breathed in the dews, dawns, rains, frosts and sunshine of the Forest, feeling the sap and surge of it pulsing through my blood until it hardly seemed to matter whether I got well or not, for to share in, to be aware of, that life of nature was itself a mode of living. I had not then read D. H. Lawrence, but his poems and early novels express much of what I felt—an almost ecstatic joy in the thrust and flux of life, in the renewal of the seasons and the renewal of generations, and even in death as part of that cycle of renewal.[27]

[23]

It is not difficult to recognize in this description many of the themes, and much of the zest, of Nicholson's poetry.

Nicholson returned to Millom in September, 1932; but his health remained extremely precarious for the next fifteen years at least, requiring a careful husbanding of time and physical effort. The resumption of formal education was out of the question, as was the taking up of any full-time job; and, since the publication of his first book in 1942, Nicholson has earned his living entirely by the various forms of his writing. Though his health improved substantially over the last two decades, not until 1965 did the last traces of tuberculosis disappear.

The effect of the two years spent enjoying the "winds and mists and sounds and smells of Hampshire" was to make Nicholson feel "a thorough-bred countryman," and so it is not surprising to find that his initial reaction on seeing his home town, especially a home town stagnating in the industrial depression of the 1930s, was a jaundiced one. The new alien-ness of Millom stunned him—the town seemed utterly unconnected with its natural surroundings. For the next two years, he turned his back on it, keeping away not only from the ironworks but also from the church. Avid reading of George Bernard Shaw and H. G. Wells at the sanatorium had turned him temporarily into an agnostic and a socialist who felt that the church's insistence on an apparently puritan morality and on man's fallen state was a denial of human dignity and of essential human goodness. It took Nicholson the rest of the decade, struggling the while to adjust to the restraints made necessary by his illness and to overcome a sense of futility in his life, to reach a solidly based Christianity and a sense of the value and meaning of his local environment—to learn, in fact, those lessons which a reading of his poetry by itself might suggest were easily attained.

From 1934 onwards, negative attitudes began gradually to be displaced. In that year Nicholson discovered the poetry of T. S. Eliot—not the Eliot of "Ash Wednesday" but the apparently disillusioned Eliot of *The Waste Land.* The sheer power of its language had the shock effect for him of "a stinging nettle accidentally grasped,"[28] and the poem's ability to make sense of a disjointed world led him to realize that his own industrial environment could be seen as part of a pattern. One feels, briefly, that the tone of the poem was morally bracing for Nicholson—it stimulated him to look more courageously at his own superficially depressing surroundings:

[24]

It was Mr. Eliot...who made us aware of the meadow behind the muckheap, who pointed out the significance of the dilapidated school and the empty church on the hill. It was not a very hopeful picture that he made of it, but at twenty years of age, we did not bother much about hope... indeed, we found despair quite exhilarating. What mattered was that suddenly everything in our world had its meaning. The most disparate events and objects took on a new relation to each other, becoming allegorical while remaining themselves.[29]

The ability to relate "disparate objects" was further encouraged by Nicholson's interest in wild flowers. At first, he studied these in "natural" surroundings of a conventional rural sort; but to find the rarer species he had to hunt among the abandoned workings of the iron-ore mines. This search drew his eye back to the town, and he came to realize that it, too, was a part of nature: "I saw that the black-headed gulls nested just as happily among the slagbanks and old rubble tips as they did on the sand-dunes at Ravenglass, and if the incongruity of the site did not bother them, why should it bother me?"[30]

Another positive influence was Sir James Frazer's *The Golden Bough,* which Nicholson had read as a result of his reading *The Waste Land*. Frazer's study of ancient fertility cults, with their ritual of the killing of the priest-king, drew Nicholson's attention to the parallelism between Christ's death and resurrection and the cyclical decay and rebirth of the year. He began to see religion not as "a puritan, bourgeois, life-denying morality"[31] riddled with prohibitions but as something centered on a necessary dying in order to live.

In these vital years of adjustment and self-discovery, three friendships[32] had particular importance for Nicholson. The first was with a young woman called Bessie Satterthwaite, who had been a classmate at Millom Secondary School. When she went to Manchester University in 1933 to read English, she and Nicholson spent much of her vacations discussing literature and his own earliest poems. Her Christian faith was an encouragement to Nicholson in his own strivings after religious belief, and it was through her that he first met the Reverend (later Canon) Samuel Taylor. Taylor had come to Millom in about 1935 to be vicar of the old church of Holy Trinity, his move having been prompted by a state of poor health which must have made him especially sympathetic to Nicholson. He was no run-of-the-mill

[25]

clergyman: he was a decided socialist in his politics and both a passionate admirer, and a relation, of Aldous Huxley. From being a "patron" figure to the young would-be poet, talking freely to him and lending him books otherwise hard to obtain, he became a lifelong friend. His friendship helped to draw Nicholson back to church attendance, and by 1938 Taylor's advice was being sought on matters of religious doctrine. Nicholson's longest-lasting friendship, and the one most closely related to his career as a poet and dramatist, began in 1937. In the July of that year Bessie Satterthwaite attended a conference organized by the Student Christian Movement, and to this conference she took a batch of Nicholson's earliest poems, which she showed to Brother George Every, who was lecturing on modern poetry. Every was impressed by the vitality of the poems and by the perseverance of their author, who had struggled to poetic expression against the twin obstacles of poor health and comparative intellectual isolation. Thus began a correspondence and a friendship which proved invaluable to Nicholson in many ways.

George Every, about six years older than Nicholson, was a member of the Society of the Sacred Mission, an order of the Anglican Church which prepared young men for the ministry. He was himself a critic and poet, publishing much of his work in *The Criterion;* he had made the acquaintance of T. S. Eliot at Kelham, the headquarters of the Society, which Eliot used as a place to which he retired for periodic religious retreats. Over the years, Every criticized Nicholson's poetry, acted as a sympathetic sounding board for his ideas, suggested him as a reviewer to the editor of the *New English Weekly* (the first English national magazine to print any of Nicholson's poems), gave him a great deal of historical help in the composition of his biblical verse plays, and advised him during his gradual return to Christian belief.

One particularly encouraging form of help Every gave Nicholson was to send his poems to T. S. Eliot, who responded with what was for him a reasonable degree of approval: "I do think there is very likely something here, if he is young enough, and I am pleased by an interest in a variety of things outside himself, and a livelier experimentation with varieties of metre than is usual. It is still very unformed, of course."[33] Every arranged, in the autumn of 1938, a meeting in London between Nicholson and the poet for whom he had "an unavoidable veneration."[34] He also sent Nicholson's poems to Michael Roberts, who replied by writing Nicholson a three-page letter full of careful technical criticism in which he suggested that some poems be submitted to *Poetry* (Chicago). This suggestion resulted in the first important publication of Nicholson's poems anywhere, for in the March, 1938, issue of that magazine his poem "Song for 7 p.m." appeared. Another poem, "Sonnet for an Introvert," was printed in *Poetry* in January, 1939.

Simultaneously with Nicholson's introduction to the wider literary world, his local opportunities were broadening. In the autumn of 1938 he gave a series of lectures on the modern novel for the Millom branch of the Workers' Educational Association. The lectures were repeated in Whitehaven the following year, and Nicholson continued such work until the early years of World War II, when a number of minor hemorrhages forced him to discontinue it. These lectures formed the basis of his first critical book, *Man and Literature,* published in 1943, and the traveling involved in their delivery gave Nicholson first-hand knowledge of the Cumberland places described in his volume *Five Rivers.*

Nevertheless, the last years of the 1930s were by no means a period of unmixed improvement for him. He continued to be dogged by ill health, and it is apparent from his letters that the restrictions imposed by his physical constitution involved a good deal of mental tension, conscientiously though he tried to adjust himself to his narrowed horizons. The burden of ill health was compounded by a sense of futility: he tried to preserve his health, but to what end? Substantial publication would have provided a kind of self-justification, but he was not, despite publication in *Poetry*, gaining the degree of literary success for which he had hoped. Eliot's interest had not led to publication in *The Criterion,* to which he had sent some poems early in 1938. Geoffrey Grigson's *New Verse* had not accepted any of his work; despite "an encouraging letter"[35] from Julian Symons, neither had *Twentieth Century Verse;* the mention of Michael Roberts's name had failed to unlock the doors of *The Listener,* and the editor of *Life and Letters* had omitted even to read what Nicholson had sent. This unpromising state of affairs dragged on for two more years. A first novel, *Love to the Nth,* was rejected in 1939 by Longmans and by Chatto and Windus; and in March, 1940, T. S. Eliot drastically criticized a second unpublished novel, *The Cat's Got the Toothache,* which he had originally appeared to think was not too bad. All this lack

[27]

of success left Nicholson feeling "like a cart without a horse—or perhaps a car with a driver but without any petrol."[36]

The lack of a firm religious belief exacerbated Nicholson's depression, but the last years of the 1930s show him gradually moving towards a strength of Christian feeling akin to the intensity he had experienced for a short time after his confirmation. Though he was held back by the sense that true faith could not be forced, he knew that "only Christianity can give the stability I need,"[37] and he regularly attended services at Canon Samuel Taylor's church. But, though Nicholson believed in a God "continuously in touch with his creation,"[38] what he found for a long time hard to grasp was the historicity of the Incarnation.

Acceptance of the reality of the Incarnation did finally come to him, however, and in a way which suggests that he had been unconsciously moving towards it. While arguing religious matters with friends, Nicholson realized that he was defending, as the one concept absolutely fundamental to Christianity, the embodiment of God in "an obscurely-born Jewish child."[39] The apparent suddenness of this discovery is easier to understand when one considers the kind of person Nicholson has described himself as being, a man "literal, matter-of-fact, fond of specifications, distrustful of abstractions."[40] To such a person, already believing in God, and believing also in the importance of material reality, it must have come to seem inevitable that God should decide to manifest himself in a child born at a precise time and in a specific place. And it may be felt that the Incarnation subsequently became the foundation stone of Nicholson's belief in "the reality and purpose of *this* world."[41] Certainly a realization of Nicholson's literal acceptance of the Incarnation enables the reader to understand much more fully his interest in such aspects of the external world as birds, flowers, places, and rock formations—while "remaining themselves," all these things are also "allegorical," the earthly manifestations of the existence of God.

Nicholson's return to Christian belief was marked by his becoming again a full, communicant member of the Anglican Church, and in a poem written in October, 1940, he recorded his communion as a turning point in his life:

NOW THAT I HAVE MADE MY DECISION and felt God on my
    tongue
It is time that I trained my tongue to speak of God;
Not with pretended wisdom, not with presumption,
But as a tree might speak of him, that no resumption
Of yesterday's words may sour the sweet grapes of the blood.

Now that I have burned my boats on the ebbing sea
That once was quicksand but returned to would-be sand of hell,
It is time that I cease to stare towards the horizon for a goal,
But gear my step to the near path cogged out for my soul,
Or step if need be through the black bracken of the untracked fell.[42]

The horizon, in terms of literary success, was now, in fact, only a short
way off; and from this moment Nicholson's life gathered momentum.
From a man striving for personal equilibrium and for a meaningful
relationship with his environment, Nicholson became a poet who was
now certain of at least the Christian substratum of his work.

CHAPTER 2

Early Poetry

I N HIS guidebook *Cumberland and Westmorland,* published in 1949, Nicholson briefly describes a winter visit he had made, twenty years before, to the ancient stone circle at Swinside, a few miles into the hills north of Millom. His description indicates an awareness of menace, almost of the numinous, in his confrontation with the "black, huddled and hooded" stones,[1] which suggests that at an early age he had something of a poet's sensitivity. It was not until after his illness and early convalescence, however, that Nicholson began to write poetry. In the period from about 1937 to 1942 Nicholson wrote about thirty poems, of which a dozen appeared in magazines; but in 1942 he said in a letter to Bessie Satterthwaite that "on the whole I'm glad to destroy much of my stuff—indeed there's scarcely anything written before the war which I would now wish to preserve."[2] Nevertheless, these early poems are worth consideration, for they afford an insight into Nicholson's poetic beginnings in the socially conscious 1930s. Many of them deserved the rejections which so depressed Nicholson at the end of that decade, but others show clear signs of a lively, if often imitative, poetic talent; and a few could easily have passed muster in a volume.

I   *The Social Poetry*

The dominant image in the poetry of the 1930s is that of the sick society, and the key question is Auden's "What do you think of England, this country of ours where nobody is well?"[3] Nicholson in 1937 was equally aware of the sickness; and, though it was in accents resembling those of Auden and Day Lewis that his socially conscious poems were spoken, their actual material was in no way derivative. Nicholson's social background and his immediate industrial environment placed him in far closer personal contact with working people than the Oxford-reared social poets, despite their working-class sympathies, could lay claim to. With some justification, therefore, Nicholson defended to George Every his use of a poetic stock-in-trade of which Auden and Day Lewis might seem to have established ownership: "You can't call it affectation for me to bring mines and blast furnaces and the like into my landscape for I can see them out of the windows of my home."[4]

Only later, however, was Nicholson able to use such imagery convincingly; for his poem of November, 1937, called "Sonnet at Night," though it expresses a sincere enough wish to be identified with the iron workers of Millom, is too strained in its language. The rather affected omission of commas and the overemphatic enjambment suggest a consciously "heroic" approach, and the last line of the octave smacks strongly of the "literary fellow-traveller" aspect of many poets of the 1930s:

> Edged by diamond-hard light the chimneys bore
> Down deep into the cloudy strata of the dark.
> Along the cakewalk gangways workmen steer
> Bogeys freightened with pigiron limestone coke
> And the pencil ore of their own veins, the muscle
> Of their tensile limbs, their lungs and the skill of their
> Hands, rammed in the hell-on-earth furnace that smelts all
> All to forge the flame of the mailed future.

Despite an "unavoidable veneration" for the poetry of T. S. Eliot, Nicholson reacted more strongly at this time to the magnetism of poets closer to his own generation: "Of the younger men, Auden seems to me of incomparably the greatest stature, and most of his aims in poetry seem to be mine—I can aim at the stars even if I only succeed in hitting the galvanised iron roof. I also like MacNeice and Michael Roberts, and some Empson and MacDiarmid—poetry with edge to it."[5] As well as their "edge," what Nicholson valued in some of these poets was their popular appeal. The poetry of *The Orators* (1932) had a catchiness lacking in Eliot, and Nicholson praised Auden's "Letter to Lord Byron" (1937) because it seemed to point towards a possible future popular poetry. He approved of Louis MacNeice's verse play *Out of the Picture* (1937) for the same reason.

Despite the uncharacteristic context—a discussion of "social" poetry

[31]

of the 1930s—in which Nicholson's view "that poetry must return to the people"[6] was expressed, such a view reveals Nicholson's early awareness of poetry's need for an audience, and one of his own earliest attempts to speak directly of the ills of the time was a poem "in rather tub-thumping rhythms"[7] written in September, 1937, and called, rather quaintly, "Grip the Rock, Auntie." In its feeling, this poem might be thought of as Nicholson's version of C. Day Lewis's *The Magnetic Mountain* (1933), at least of those parts of that poem which point disgustedly at what is wrong with society. But its tone and the incantatory pattern of its four longish stanzas recall Auden's vague and sinister warnings to the middle classes (as issued, for instance, in *The Dog Beneath the Skin*[8]), and the reader may well feel that the poet is preening himself because he shares some dark and exclusive secret:

> Sniff the air, Auntie,
> With an inquisitive spaniel nose,
> Are you aware, Auntie,
> Of a faint smell of burning singeing the breeze?
> Will it compare, Auntie,
> To a bonfire stoked by mischievous boys?
> What do they care
> That there's lace on the guy as well as rags,
> And banknotes in the sawdust and money-bags,
> That the crackers are shells—it's a blaze they're after
> In the rubbish dump flared by their daredevil laughter.
>
> And isn't there, Auntie,
> A subtler stench in the smoky acid
> Like the rare
> Carrion taint of a civilisation gone bad?

Vigor and verve are well in evidence, but the poem is too much a virtuoso performance; too contrived and too rhetorical, its attitude betrays arrogance and immaturity—for the poet, too, is part of the society at which he preaches.

The long poem "By the Sea," written at about the same time, takes a more sympathetic stance; though more awkward and involuted in expression than "Grip the Rock, Auntie," it is more impressive because it is based on a real experience of Nicholson's local environment. The landscape is partly an imagined waste land but partly Millom as well, and, though Nicholson's description of the unemployed owes a great deal to Eliot's "Choruses of the Unemployed" in *The Rock* (1934), the

unemployed themselves are actual local people with whose lives
Nicholson was personally involved:

> But among sand-blocked wharves and stagnant docks
>   The metal waters rust,
> And crank up and down like an old chain swaying in the wind
>   From a derelict lobster-armed crane.
> And stepping over worm-eaten sleepers, past the walls
>   Of the silent foundry, come the
>   men with hands in pockets
>   humpbacked to the world,
>   locked out of mine and mill
>   by a machine by an explosion by a jump
>   in prices by a change in fashion
>   by a director's whim by a slump
>   in a glutted world by a poverty-
>   strangled demand by investor's
>   mumps by a war by a peace
>   by profits by corners by swindlers
>   by deals scoops ramps threats lies,
>   . . . .
>   now father dependent on son
>   brother on brother man
>   on men unknown, hands
>   reft of pickaxe and spade
>   grudgingly take the dole
>   of another man's hewing and digging.

Apart from "By the Sea," whose social commentary is underpinned
by strivings for religious belief and by a direct awareness of
unemployment in a painstakingly realized local environment,
Nicholson's "political" poems of 1937 are tributes to the widely felt
urgencies of their time and to the influence of that era's "social" poets,
rather than milestones in his own development. Aside from "Prayer for
a Political Meeting" (1939), where fingermarks of Auden's "Sir, no
man's enemy" and "Spain" are accompanied by a metrical pattern
reminiscent of Eliot's choruses in *The Rock,* there is nothing in the
"social poetry" vein later than 1937. More significant indications of
development are found in the personal poems which Nicholson began
to write in that year and which comprise the major part of his output in
1938.

II *Personal Poems*

The year 1937 produced the twin poems "Poem in Pencil" and "Poem in Ink," love poems which use a type of short line already made familiar by Auden. [9] "Poem in Ink" draws parallels between bread and woman's flesh, human love and Communion; and it begins with a simultaneous awareness of natural raw material and human product which anticipates such later poems as "Rock Face" in its implication of the close relationship between man and nature:

> The knife in the loaf
> Saws into the sheaf,
> The crisp sheaf bundled
> Like firewood on my table.
> . . . .
> The analyst teeth
> Pestle the bread
> To elemental sun
> And oxidised corn.

This same meter was used in May, 1938, for "Poem before Pentecost," which Nicholson sent in vain to John Middleton Murry, the editor of *The Adelphi*. The poem exhibits a grace of movement and a naturalness of language, and it also indicates Nicholson's religious problem at the time—his need for God to take the initiative which he was unable to take himself:

> The love in our blood
> Cannot burn the flaked skin,
> Is choked from within
> For lack of air.
> Come love from above
> And scorch us bare,
> That spring may burst
> From our budding blood
> With the flare of the first bracken,
> With the fire of God.

The same grace and freshness of language is found in "The Wind and the Window," written July 5, 1938. The need expressed in this poem is that of realizing the objective existence of the outside world. The poem's questions suggest that Nicholson is not satisfied with the possible solipsism of fancy but will only see a meaning in the world if he can believe that it will survive his own death. As well as by its subject the reader's attention is caught by the unobtrusive skill of the poem's technique, its easy manipulation of an invented stanza:

> Tell me, Window, all the wonder
> Of the bobbined, winding hours,
> People cut from cardboard, spellbound,
> Prams and pigeons and torn flowers,
> Puppet pageant of the street,
> Is it truth or is it sleight?
> Eyes that sift the light
> Tell, if you can tell.

> When my breath is broken, Wind, oh
> When my sight is shuttered too,
> Will you blow, Wind? Window, will you
> Open still to others' view?
> Or are noises in the street
> Only echoes of my note?
> Flickerings of fate—
> Breath upon the sill.

Renewed religious faith gave Nicholson the basis for belief in "the reality. . . of *this* world" and, when he outlined in 1949 his attitude to poetic imagery, he in effect gave his own answer to the questions he had asked in "The Wind and the Window" eleven years before: "The first article of faith for me as a poet is a complete and unreserved belief in the objective reality of the world around me, and in the general trustworthiness of my senses to inform me about that world. I realize, of course, that my picture of the world must be modified by the limits both of those senses and of the brain which interprets them, but this does not prevent me from believing that my experience, however incomplete it may be, is still an experience of something which has a real existence outside and independent of me."[10]

"The Wind and the Window" may be seen, therefore, not as the lyrical meandering of a young poet but as the statement of a serious philosophical question, the later answer to which is one of the keys to an understanding of the profoundly factual nature of Nicholson's poetry, its detailed dwelling on the world of nature, its precise naming of flowers, and its accurate use of proper geological terminology.

It was not, however, by such lyrical poems as the three just commented on that Nicholson's work was represented in literary magazines at this time. The two poems which appeared in *Poetry*, "Song for 7 p.m." and "Sonnet for an Introvert," are contorted, self-conscious, and "literary." "Song for 7 p.m." draws far too much attention to its style, and it suggests a self-absorbed savoring of unfamiliar words and a too-conscious use of technical tricks:

> Call to the coiled night slowly to unfurl
> Its fronded secrets; here in the cool cowled cloisters of the evening
> Call to the winds to uncluster
> From the voluted ear the conchoid curls.

The sonnet reveals an overstrained rhetoric which overtook Nicholson whenever he used that particular form: fortunately, he was soon to abandon it. The parallel construction and portentous alliteration of the last line create a theatrical air which reduces sympathy for the emotional problem hinted at:

> Buttress my limbs against the corrosion of
> The dry rot at the heart, the crumbling nerves,
> Against the explosion of the grenade love
> Which cracks the brittle facade of reserve.
> Bolt fast my body, seal from roof to toe;
> What others do not see I need not know.

Both these poems reveal that Nicholson was tempted to "bare his soul," a habit which in his mature poetry he is far from indulging in. That he was aware of the dangers of posturing inherent in such a confessional manner shows clearly in a remark he made in 1938 about Dylan Thomas, a poet whose technical skill and verbal fluency he otherwise greatly admired: "His introversive twining of words around himself irritates me almost to the extent of disgusting me. He represents, in a highly-developed form, what I do not want from poetry, and the direction of his work is the one which I feel the poetry of the immediate future must at all costs avoid."[11] By 1940 Nicholson had decided strongly that such pitfalls, at least, were not for him: "The introspective element in my earlier work I am now seeking to eradicate."[12]

III   *The Maturing Poet*

By and large, Nicholson's most characteristic work stresses not the more private elements in his experience but those capable of general application. The urge is to communicate rather than simply to express. In the late 1930s Nicholson turned to a use of symbols, particularly "the symbols of the journey and the search,"[13] and to the use of pseudorealistic narrative that had the force of archetypal myth in an attempt to express his own feelings in a way which would involve those of his readers. In three poems written in 1938—the unpublished "The Headless Horse," together with "Burning Tarn" and "No Man's Land" (published in the American magazine *The Southern Review* in 1942 and 1940, respectively)—Nicholson attempts to fuse the literalness of local detail with a deeper appeal to the imagination and to find a language which expresses the spiritual dimensions of human experience.

The theme of all three poems is human doubt and fear of something "unknown," and the poems are all influenced by Kafka, on whom Nicholson had been lecturing at this time.[14] "The Headless Horse" and "Burning Tarn" do not really succeed, and their obscurity seems to derive from a lack of clarity in the poet's own thinking. Despite the undeniable fact that uncertainty is a basic element in these poems, it is still irritating not to be able to establish a reasonably distinct meaning for their symbolic titles. "No Man's Land" is far more successful, perhaps because the sense of the "unknown" which it conveys emerges from a more sharply aural and visual presentation of landscape.

"No Man's Land" is written in spare, tense quatrains reminiscent of Auden's early "telegraphese" style:

> I have heard crack the warning
> Ice, alone,
> By the debated track
> Scotched on bare stone.
>
> I have traversed the salient,
> Been aware of
> The cairn beyond the next cairn,
> The menace in a sheep's cough:
>
> The snaring bog,
> The threat of nightfall,
> The sniper's cue
> In the snipe's call.

The last two lines are more than a piece of clever verbal economy: "the snipe's call" could easily be a man in ambush. But there is an unmistakable echo of Auden's "Missing": "Hear curlew's creaking call/ From angles unforeseen,/ The drumming of a snipe,"[15] and there is the same threatening atmosphere that is found in Auden's " 'O where are you going?' said reader to rider."[16] Similarity, however, is not necessarily pastiche: all that can fairly be said is that just as Auden's "social" poetry probably revealed to Nicholson the contemporary significance of his home town, so Auden's references to the bleak North-country landscape may have made Nicholson realize the poetic potential of certain types of Cumbrian scenery. In fact, "No Man's Land" is rooted in an experience which preceded Nicholson's reading of Auden: his visit, at the age of fifteen, to Swinside stone circle, which was mentioned at the beginning of this chapter.[17] The sense of an unknown presence behind what is seen is rendered with vivid immediacy; short, staccato phrases reproduce with uncanny mimicry the pricking-up of ears and the sharpening of vision of a man in the act of registering an extra dimension just beyond the range of his senses:

> What is it?
> What is there?
> At bay on startled heels,
> I challenge the blank air.
>
> Stockstill. Take my bearings. I know
> Every quarry in the valley, every chock
> —stone in the gulley, every gutter in the ghyll. . .
> I do not know that rock.

During Nicholson's five years, from 1937 to 1942, of apprentice work in poetry, comparatively few of his poems achieved publication; and those which did either appeared in English magazines of small literary influence or were hidden in American magazines whose importance was counteracted by the difficulty involved in procuring them in England. Nicholson's first significant opportunity of reaching an audience occurred in 1943. The firm of John Bale and Staples was intending to issue a small volume of *Selected Poems* by Keith Douglas, J. C. Hall, and Alan Rook (now mainly remembered for his anthology piece "Dunkirk Pier"[18]). When Alan Rook was offered separate publication elsewhere, twelve poems by Nicholson (eight of them

[38]

reprinted in *Five Rivers* the following year) filled the space left vacant. Keith Douglas was to come into his own later with his maturer war poems, but at the time *Selected Poems* appeared Nicholson received most of the favorable critical attention given to the volume. Stephen Spender, among others, singled him out as "much the most skilful"[19] of the three poets.

The only early poem which Nicholson printed in this volume was "The Blackberry," written September 17, 1939. It is worth examining in some detail, as it is the first poem to show Nicholson's emergence from a would-be poet's trial-and-error into both a manner and a theme characteristically his. A short poem, it can conveniently be quoted in full:

> Between the railway and the mine,
> Brambles are in fruit again.
> > Their little nigger fists they clench,
> > And hold the branches in a clinch.
>
> Waggons of ore are shunted past,
> And spray the berries with red dust,
> > Which dulls the bright mahogany
> > Like purple sawdust clogged and dry.
>
> But when the housewife, wind and rain,
> Rubs the berry spick and span,
> > Compound it gleams like a fly's eye,
> > And every ball reflects the sky.
>
> There the world's reflected like
> Coupons in a ration book;
> > There the tall curved chimneys spread
> > Purple smoke on purple cloud.
>
> Grant us to know that hours rushed by
> Are photographed upon God's eye;
> > That life and leaf are both preserved
> > In gelatine of Jesus' blood.
>
> And grant to us the sense to feel
> The large condensed within the small;
> > Wash clear our eyes that we may see
> > The sky within the blackberry.

The first impression is of a modest homeliness, but the well-known theme (recalling William Blake's "infinity in a grain of sand") is made vivid by unexpected words like *nigger* and *gelatine* which are immediately striking. Colloquialisms like "spick and span" and the topical image of the ration book give the poem a degree of freshness which many reviewers commented upon favorably when *Five Rivers* appeared in 1944.[20]

The poem's precise handling of octosyllabic couplets is reminiscent of Andrew Marvell, and a closer inspection reveals a method of composition which may be likened to that of Metaphysical poetry. The images are in effect conceits and, in that they are occasionally pushed too far, conceits in a slightly pejorative sense. Nicholson is not, for instance, content with the phrase "nigger fists:" instead of leaving the metaphor of boxing to be inferred beneath the "color" denotation, he brings it to the surface in the phrase "in a clinch," and the attempt to be "witty" results in a picture which, unusual for Nicholson, is not quite an accurate description of the natural object. The later comparison of the many-faceted blackberry to a "fly's eye" (1. 11) is reasonable in itself; but it has unsuitable repercussions when, farther on, the blackberry becomes "God's eye," which records life and the passing of time as the blackberry itself mirrors the "tall curved chimneys." A more important objection is raised by lines nineteen and twenty; for in what sense, exactly, are "life and leaf" (the world of man and the world of nature) "preserved" in "Jesus' blood"? The theological meaning is presumably that Christ has redeemed the world from destruction by dying for it. The "gelatine" image, however, suggests the "fixing" of something in a state of stillness—a kind of aspic. The reader may suspect that "preserved" has been associated in the poet's subconscious with "preserves" (jam), and that this association has in its turn suggested fruit jelly at a child's Sunday tea. An obscure pun seems to have clouded what should have been a simple idea.[21]

A certain verbal self-indulgence also characterized such early poems as "May Day 1937" and even "By the Sea," so that to claim that "The Blackberry" inaugurates a completely new and flawless style would be an exaggeration. Nevertheless, the religious theme of "The Blackberry" seems to have been more congenial to Nicholson's temperament than his earlier attempts at poetic social commitment; and the flaws of this particular poem do not greatly detract from its vividness and ability to please: its language and imagery are more under control, and both subserve a developing sense of structure.

Perhaps the most significant aspect of "The Blackberry" is the way in which it works forward from a small detail, and a local setting, to a large conclusion. The method underscores the subject—the finding of wider significance in something which might ordinarily go unnoticed, the discovery of "the sky within the blackberry." The idea of this early poem is essentially the same as is demonstrated, with commensurately greater individuality and personal relevance, in the poem "The Pot Geranium" of a decade later, in which Nicholson sees in his local environment a microcosm of the world. It is thus possible broadly to agree with an account which Nicholson gave of "The Blackberry" in 1964: ". . . I can clearly remember the poem which seems to me the first of my poems, the first Nicholson poem. I can remember writing it. I was out one day after the war began, and I scribbled this and I was almost imitating Herbert. I wasn't writing the sort of poem which I wanted to write, and it wasn't till some months after that, that I found that I had begun to write without knowing it. I had begun to write in the way I was going to write."[22]

CHAPTER 3

Volumes of Poetry (1944-1954)

NORMAN NICHOLSON published six volumes of poetry up to the
end of the 1960s, but with only three of them—*Five Rivers*
(1944), *Rock Face* (1948), and *The Pot Geranium* (1954)—need critical
study concern itself. Eight of the poems in *Selected Poems* (1943) were
reprinted in *Five Rivers;* the four omitted[1] are of little interest and are
certainly no better than a number of earlier poems which, by that time,
Nicholson had allowed to vanish. The *Selected Poems* of 1966 includes
no new poems but the collection demonstrates the poet's predilection
for his later work[2] and incorporates a number of small textual changes.
No Star on the Way Back, a pamphlet printed in Manchester in 1967, is
religious occasional verse, consisting of ballads and carols taken from a
Christmas play written for television in 1963.

Each of the three volumes to be considered has its own individual
flavor and represents broadly a distinct phase in Nicholson's poetic
development, but it is also possible to discern clear thematic links
between all three of them. All deal with basic Nicholsonian
themes—Man and God, and the relationship between Man and his
physical environment—but it may be said that, whereas in *Five Rivers*
(and, to a lesser degree, in *Rock Face*), regional and religious themes
tend to be treated separately, in *The Pot Geranium* they are fused in an
awareness—often overtly stated—of the underlying unity of Man and
the God-created world in which he lives. Throughout the three volumes
may be traced Nicholson's growing ability to let the rhythms of speech
rather than that of "verse" shape his poems and to prune back an
undergrowth of metaphor and conceit to allow "the meaning of the
object itself"[3] to show through clearly.

The three volumes share a common pattern of organization. The title
poem comes first, as if Nicholson wished to strike unmistakably what
was for him the dominant note of each volume. Almost invariably, the
last poems are the longest and most ambitious. Within this framework,

the poems are grouped according to subject or type—"regional," "Biblical," "lyrical," "philosophical," "religious," and so on. Nicholson's own presentation of his poems has suggested the adoption of a thematic approach to them.

I Five Rivers

In 1943, Nicholson submitted a collection of poems to M. J. Tambimuttu, the editor of the very influential magazine *Poetry London.* Tambimuttu rejected the collection; and, at the suggestion of Anne Ridler (then T. S. Eliot's secretary), whom Nicholson had first met during his visit to London in 1938, it was then offered for consideration to Faber and Faber. Impressed by the coherence of the collection, Eliot responded favorably; and *Five Rivers* was published in 1944. Despite its occasional echoes of Eliot, the volume shows an impressive degree of originality; and even its touches of overexuberance only reinforce the general impression which it gives of great vitality and colorfulness of language. The originality is, in part, simply a question of subject matter: Nicholson's discovery of the poetic potential of his own region makes itself apparent from the start in the local place names which provide the titles for his first eight poems. The three long biblical poems at the end of the volume are set in an obviously Cumbrian landscape, as is the group of poems which present Nicholson's response to the pressures of World War II and thus root the volume firmly in a particular time as well as in a particular place.

The place is presented in very general terms in the title poem, "Five Rivers":

> Southward from Whitehaven, where cliffs of coal
> Slant like shale to the low black mole,
> The railway canters along the curving shore
> Over five rivers, which slowly pour
> On the steps of the shingle where the grey gulls bask:
> EHEN and CALDER, IRT and MITE and ESK.

The very straightforwardness of this descriptive opening is striking. The poem aroused comment when it first appeared because landscape description was not a prevailing fashion in the 1940s, and this poem is almost entirely descriptive. Nicholson's confidence in the attractions of his own region is attested by the poem's use of the third person, by the naive-sounding loose couplets, and most of all by the fact that he should have written the poem. The vivacity of its language is sufficient reason for its existence.

The poem's description is not so much directly visual as the imaginative simplification of an area. The printing of the river names in capitals suggests that the poem may most easily be likened to a sort of Baedeker's Guide, and their listing in north to south order sends the reader to look at a map. A descriptive detail like ". . . the channels burst through a gap in the sand/ Like a three-pronged pitchfork jabbed in the flank of the land" implies a landscape seen from above rather than as a series of still-lifes framed by the ordinary terrestrial eye. The poem may also be likened to a travelogue; the rivers supply the bare minimum of organization, and each gives rise to its own kind of picture. The Ehen runs red with "the blood of the ore/ Of the mines of Egremont and Cleator Moor." The Calder prompts the poet to reconstruct in his mind the life of the now-ruined abbey past which it flows. The Irt recalls a scrap of local folklore and the former local spinner of tall stories, Will Ritson. The River Mite simply provides an excuse for a playful and punning sketch of the Ravenglass and Eskdale Light Railway:

> The MITE, the tyke, lollops along
> Like a blue-haired collie with a dribbling tongue,
> The children's plaything as they ride the toy train
> That runs beneath the rocks in a hawthorn lane,
> Where dog-daisy, dogrose and stiff dog-grass
> Bark at the wheels as the whistling truckloads pass.

The flexibility of the couplets gives the poem a light-hearted, impromptu air, so that Nicholson is easily enabled to string together visual impressionism, verbal fantasy, history, and economics. The last lines strike with brief, nostalgic poignancy a more "romantic" posture, which, in keeping with the poem's general unpretentiousness, relapses into the inconsequential:

> Brown clouds are blown against the bright fells
> Like Celtic psalms from drowned Western isles.
> The slow rain falls like memory
> And floods the becks and flows to the sea,
> And there on the coast of Cumberland mingle
> The fresh and the salt, the cinders and the shingle.

The most serious lines in "Five Rivers" describe "the mines of Egremont and Cleator Moor," where "drill and navvy break the stone/ And hack the living earth to the bone," and suggest Nicholson's awareness of the hard economics of Cumberland as well as of its tourist attractions. In the two poems immediately following "Five Rivers," Nicholson works out this idea in more detail; he shows that, for him, the phrase "the living earth" is no facile anthropomorphic tag but embodies a truth which needs to be realized if man is to organize his life sanely. These poems contain the presentation of a theme which reverberates through Nicholson's work: the correct relationship between man and the earth out of which he extracts a living.

In contrast to the suitable looseness of "Five Rivers," the poems "Egremont" and "Cleator Moor" employ tight octosyllabic couplets and a high proportion of half-rhymes to give an edge of emphasis and an appropriately ironic inflection to their statements. "Egremont" begins with a lyricism reminiscent of Tennyson's line "The splendour falls on castle walls":

> November sunlight floats and falls
> Like soapsuds on the castle walls.
> Where broken groins are slanted west
> The bubbles touch the stone and burst,
> And the moist shadows dribble down
> And slime the sandy red with brown.

The extension, characteristic of Nicholson at this time, of the "soapsud" simile into a conceit and the three ensuing stanzas describing the castle's history deceive the reader into thinking that the poem is simply a picture of the "romantic," Border-ballad past. The fifth and sixth stanzas turn the literal Egremont castle upside-down: it becomes a metaphor for the modern iron mines where "With lantern flints the miners spark/ And gouge their windows to the dark." But the poem is more than a clever ironic contrasting of the past with the "sordid" industrial present in which man is reduced to a sort of digging animal. The poem's real point emerges in stanza seven, which reveals the true past whose rapine and murder are equivalent to the modern "theft from earth" which, in Nicholson's view, mining has become. But the poem is a trifle let down by its apocalyptic, *deus-ex-machina* ending; though Nicholson is aware of an evil, he does not render it with contemporary immediacy; he substitutes for a realistic solution a convenient local legend:[4]

> But the robbed earth will claim its own
> And break the mines and castle down
> When Gabriel from heaven sent
> Blows the horn of Egremont,
> Tabulates the tenants' needs
> And re-assumes the title deeds.

Of this first group of poems in *Five Rivers,* "Cleator Moor" is much the most successful; one of Nicholson's best poems, it is trenchant, concise, and moving. With the terse energy of a border ballad its quatrains describe three stages in the history of local mining: early prosperity when both coal and iron were dug from the same shaft; the slump of the 1930s when "we saw the disgusting absurdity of huge stocks of coal which nobody would buy, while the local people had to gather sticks on the shore for fuel";[5] and the revitalization of local mining brought about, ironically, by the wartime demand for armaments. Nicholson was horrified by the fact that Cleator Moor, which in a letter of 1938 he had described as "a mortuary," should owe its new lease of life to the killing of others. The perversion of man's proper relationship to the earth is emphasized by the change from stanza one's harvest imagery—"Black and red currants on one tree"—into the brutal facts of stanza seven:

> Every waggon of cold coal
> Is fire to drive a turbine wheel;
> Every knuckle of soft ore
> A bullet in a soldier's ear.

In "Cleator Moor" the poet has no need to point a moral. The facts speak for themselves, and the starkness and bite of the lines convey ample indignation. At first sight, the final stanza may seem to descend into rhetoric and cliché:

> The miner at the rockface stands,
> With his segged and bleeding hands
> Heaps on his head the fiery coal,
> And feels the iron in his soul.

Yet, more closely considered, the last couplet is far from a lax adoption of dead metaphors: the iron and coal are real, and the poem describes a situation which reanimates the "clichés" and gives them a striking inevitability. Some feeling of moral guilt is likely to be suffered by those whose renewed prosperity is due to the repugnant necessities of war.

"Cleator Moor," written about 1941, indicates that Nicholson's awareness of his region was sharpened by the war. The topical nature of *Five Rivers* is most evident in a group of poems, including among others "Fo. Anne and Alison," "Eskmeals 1943," and "Waiting for Spring 1943," which show Nicholson as reacting to war both as a Cumbrian and as a Christian. The three constituents—local setting, wartime context, and religious feeling—of what may be termed Nicholson's "war poetry" are most impressively fused in "For St. James 1943." The setting is St. George's Square, Millom; and the evidence of wartime is unobtrusively present:

> The last clinkers of sunset are strewn on the hill;
> The mist is blown about the town like smoke.
> Girls stand in the street in the brown dusk
> Talking to soldiers, and the swifts still
> Wire their screaming spirals round the market clock.

In this peaceful moment (tinged with premonition, however, by the screaming swifts), a calm religious faith is readily found: "Now we are able to take the cup./ The purple evening is like holy wine;/ We drink in grace and feel the spirit near." The transition in the next stanza, in which Nicholson turns to the difficulty of maintaining faith that is experienced by those elsewhere being bombed, is made smoother by the ambiguities of "cup" and "purple": Holy Communion and Gethsemane; the royal color and that of the robe mockingly given to Christ before his crucifixion. An equation is implied between Christ's sufferings out of which came redemption and the sufferings of man in wartime, which do not cancel out the beliefs that he holds when life is more peaceful. In the final stanza, the image of the swifts comes to represent the turning of the wheel of nature and man's eventual survival:

> Yet this evening's quiet does not deceive:
> The quiet is what endures. The swifts fly higher

[47]

> Through the drifting ash of the last light
> Into the nights of the future. And all we now believe
> Still will be true when the sky is wild with fire.

The poem ends on a heartening note of faith; but, despite the way in which this conclusion is given an air of logic by the carefully handled imagery, the poet's optimism has no self-evident grounding. "For St. James 1943" is essentially not proof but assertion; and it suggests a perennial difficulty of the religious poet: the success of his poem depends finally on a current of sympathy between himself and the reader, who must respond with at least a will to believe of his own. To a considerable degree, the lack in the twentieth century of this current of sympathy accounts for the neglect of much of Nicholson's work by critics. He once stated the problem thus: "It must sometimes appear to a young poet. . . that it is one of the greatest hindrances to literary recognition to be known as a believing Christian."[6]

Another wartime poem, "The Evacuees," presents Nicholson's equally deep belief in the importance of belonging to a particular place. The poem, which dates from 1943, tells of the influx into Millom four years earlier (during the stagnant yet uneasy period of "phoney war" which followed the German invasion of Poland) of a number of families evacuated from Newcastle-upon-Tyne on the other side of the Pennines. When the fear of imminent bombing lessened

> The women returned
> To the Tyneside husbands and the Tyneside coal,
> And most of the children followed. Others stayed and learned
> The Cumberland vowels, took strangers for their friends,
> Went home for holidays at first, then not at all,
> Accepted in the aisle the bishop's hands,
> Won scholarships and badges, and were known
> One with the indigenous children of the town.

With these "others" Nicholson is concerned; they are now teenagers, and need to find their place in the world. Can it be enough for them to remain in a town which is only their second home?

> Will they rest,
> Will they be contented, these
> Fledglings of a cuckoo's egg, reared in a stranger's nest?

Born of one people, with another bred,
Will they return to their parents again, or choose
The foster-home, or seek the unrented road?
Grant that in the future they may find
A rock on which to build a house for heart and mind.

The antithesis in the fourth line and the gravity of tone suggest that, for the poet, acclimatization to a new environment would be an unlikely solution. The objection that the stanza may well raise is that the older poet, whose particular circumstances obliged him to put down roots in his own town, is imposing upon the children's lives a problem which might seem of little moment for them. But for Nicholson the problem is a very real one; for him, its solution can only be "the unity of the breed, of the clan, of fledglings hatched in the same nest."[7]

The goodwill of the attitude conveyed by "The Evacuees" is patent; though it may prompt an objection to its basic, unargued assumption that rootedness in one's "home town" is vital, the poem renders its subject with a moving simplicity. It also indicates Nicholson's developing ability to describe events in something like a plain-speaking voice and without resorting to obvious moralizing. The issue of the children's future is left unresolved, and the slight lameness of the poem's ending represents the victory of honest uncertainty over an occasional earlier tendency to sum things up with a rhetorical inflation.

The "rock" referred to in the poem's last line represents the sense of rootedness, of belonging to a particular place. But in turning away from "telling the reader" and making what is for him the natural gesture of "asking God," Nicholson reveals clearly the other rock, that of religion, on which his own life is based. The largest single group of poems in *Five Rivers* not only shows a religious attitude but deals explicitly with Christian themes; and this group of poems is the distinguishing feature of the volume. In his later work, Nicholson expresses his religious views more obliquely in terms of natural imagery, especially the imagery of rock which is examined in such a poem as "The Seven Rocks" primarily for its own sake and which yields only secondarily a metaphorical application. In *Five Rivers*, Nicholson's beliefs seek direct expression; and, in view of the problems of the Christian poet in the twentieth century, it is interesting to see how Nicholson presents this aspect of himself.

This very phrase—"how Nicholson presents"—in itself hints at the nature of the problem. Elizabeth Jennings, in her book *Christianity and Poetry,* has stated succinctly Nicholson's problem: "What is unique about this age is the fact that the really Christian poets have had to be rebels. Christian culture has always continued, in however quiet a way, but the twentieth century has been more interested in Marxism, existentialism and Communism than in any other philosophy."[8] T. S. Eliot had expressed the situation with specific reference to writers in *After Strange Gods:* "... amongst writers the rejection of Christianity—Protestant Christianity—is the rule rather than the exception."[9] Nicholson, writing at length about the dilemma of the Christian poet in the article "Tell It Out Among the Heathen" (1956), said that the result of the Christian poet's awareness of being in a minority is that he becomes "self-conscious about his faith" and "begins to calculate its possible effect on the reader." Nevertheless, at the end of the article Nicholson repudiates, on behalf of other Christian poets as well as himself, any inference that they are "all the time consciously and deliberately setting out to preach, to explain, to persuade."[10]

A very small number of Nicholson's religious poems in *Five Rivers,* like "Gethsemane" and "The Ride to Jerusalem," are unselfconsciously devotional. Christian belief is assumed by the poet, who is quietly concerned with his own imperfect relationship to God: the reader may pass on, or participate, as he pleases. The last stanza of "The Ride to Jerusalem" illustrates the tone adopted:

> The window-sills are empty; no crowds wait;
> Here at the pavement's edge I watch alone.
> Master, like sunlight strike my slaty heart
> And ask not acclamations from the stone.

When the Christian poet wishes to present matters of theology or religious tradition, he must meet the modern reader halfway. He takes on more of a public voice; and, whether he uses parable or direct statement, his poetry is closer to the devices of the sermon than to the intimate utterances of prayer. Nicholson's view (which lies behind his choice of poems for inclusion in his 1942 *Anthology of Religious Verse*) is that the Christian poet must "re-state the Christian faith in the language and imagery of our time."

One poem in which he does so successfully is "The Preachers,"

which uses parable to show the difference between the innocence of
birds and the sinfulness of fallen man. The stanzas are terse and
pointed, and the crudity of some of the phrasing bears the same
relation to a serious theological truth as a gargoyle does to the grandeur
of a Gothic cathedral. St. Francis is depicted retelling the story of
Adam and Eve to the birds:

> The juice was sweet
>> But tart the core,
> No herb in field
>> Their gripes could cure.
> . . . .
> Tits trapezed
>> Upon the spouts,
> Starlings dropped lime
>> Like marguerites.
>
> They said to the saint
>> With scornful beak:
> "The berries give *us*
>> No bellyache."

St. Francis's sermon is neatly thrown back at him by his
"congregation," and the dramatic framework of the poem enables its
theological point to be made with wit and economy.

A longer example of a "doctrinal" poem, in which contemporaneity
is supplied by setting as well as by language, is "The Council of the
Seven Deadly Sins." In this poem the traditional vices are personified as
members of a local parish council, and the poem is an allegory rather in
the manner of William Langland, for each sin is suggested mainly by
means of physical caricature. The portrait of Gluttony is painted in
very general terms; and the satire, though exaggerated, has considerable
gusto:

> The fourth good governor has eyes
> Purple with blood and dull with booze,
> Red as ripe strawberries, his lip
> Slobbers with juice like dripping tap.
> Down his throat he'd quickly swill
> The bitter sea if it were ale,
> And, gluttonous as fire, he'd eat

> The sand if it were sausage meat,
> And stuff Scawfell inside his belly
> If it were lamb and currant jelly.

The setting in which the parish council meets is a town mysteriously covered in sand, so that "the little dunes like molehills rear/ Day by day in the town square", which seems meant to suggest the destructive effects produced in a particular context by man's timeless vices. Although the individual portraits have a crude effectiveness, the poem as a whole does not quite succeed as allegory: on a realistic level, drifting sand seems an implausible result of human sin.

Not surprisingly, for a poet who is also a Christian, Nicholson has found much of his material in the Bible. His Methodist upbringing ensured that he was as familiar with "the mythical land of Palestine" as he was with is own part of Cumberland. When he was about fourteen, the "two countries" came together: "I remember that my uncle, who was a Sunday School teacher, gave us a lesson on the Good Samaritan. 'A certain man', he said, 'went down from Jerusalem to Jericho, just as it might have been from Broughton to Foxfield.' "[11] This homely illustration suddenly "condensed and solidified" the imagined landscape of the Bible and gave it sharp local relevance. The last group of religious poems to be examined—those based on biblical stories or incidents—attempt to transmit this same relevance and contemporary application.

Two of the historical poems show how Nicholson handles his source material with different degrees of success. "Babylon" is based on the destruction of Babylon described in Revelation xviii; its last two lines are direct quotation, and the poem leads to this conclusion by describing the voyage of merchant ships laden with goods for sale in Babylon. The poem's opening is colorful and breezy, and its rhythm suitably buoyant:

> The wind was bright when we left the trading isles,
> The sun was keen as a western gale; our keel
> Cut like a saw the rolling logs of the sea.
> Porpoise bounced in the waves' blue shavings,
> And the gulls followed our decks as they follow a plough.

The voyage, of course, is imaginary, the building up of a context (perhaps influenced by Eliot's "The Journey of the Magi") in which the discovery of burning Babylon can have a considerable shock effect. The ship's hold, however, is far from containing the sort of stock-in-trade associated with the biblical Babylon; and this tends to make the fall of Babylon in the poem seem undeserved; and the quotation at the end sounds compassionate rather than exultant. Nicholson's embroidery of his source conveys no particular contemporary "message," and thus the poem seems to exist because Nicholson saw in the Bible passage an opportunity for descriptive writing for its own sake.

A more satisfying, though less exciting, poem is "The Raven," whose source is the single verse (I Kings xvii:6) which tells of the feeding of Elijah by ravens. In the poem, Nicholson recreates and improvises on this episode; he sets the poem in the Cumberland landscape which he knows firsthand and which he also was to use as the location for his play about Elijah, *The Old Man of the Mountains:*

> The raven flew down the long wedge of the dale,
> Above the upland dykes and slate and cobble walls
> Piled against the high waves of the fells.
> With slower corrugations of its wings
> It dropped below the bracken cut for bedding
> To where green oats were sown on the brant fell,
> And the lyle herdwicks fed in the wet pastures
> For the grass was thicker there and orchards and burnet grew.

The slight touch of dialect ("brant" means "steep"), and the mention of specifically Cumbrian sheep ("herdwicks"), give the poem an air of precision; but the pastoral imagery itself has a universality suited to its biblical subject. More importantly for the poem's total coherence, Nicholson's choice of a local setting ensures consistency in the imagery instead of the unevenness evident in "Babylon" and even more in its companion piece "Belshazzar." Nicholson's inclusion of "The Raven" in *Selected Poems* (1966) suggests that he himself is well aware that his real strength as a poet emerges when he composes his picture from details chosen from a known landscape rather than when his imagination tries to work on disparate and second-hand information.

The last three poems in the volume—"The Garden of the Innocent," "The Holy Mountain," and "The Bow in the Cloud"—are long, ambitious ones. They attempt to deal with the fundamental Christian myths presented in the Book of Genesis. Nicholson described the usefulness to him of myth in 1956; it was "... the common ground on which Christian and non-Christian could converse. The Garden of Eden, the Fall, the Flood. . .—these were seen to have a universal significance which could be perceived and acknowledged by those who did not accept the Christian doctrines."[12] These particular myths correspond to secular views of man as a creature nostalgic for an unattainable, or lost, perfection; as a creature aware of the dichotomy of body and spirit; and as a creature whose relationship to nature is variously that of master and victim. Nicholson's three poems are able, therefore, to some extent to communicate on both Christian and secular levels; but the Old Testament material of "The Holy Mountain" and "The Bow in the Cloud" is strongly in evidence, and much of their language is modeled on that of the Bible. All three poems, however, gain immediacy from being located in a Cumberland landscape that is described in loving detail: since adolescence Nicholson had visualized the myths of Genesis as being enacted in his own immediate area.[13]

The poems' ambitiousness of conception is matched by their ambitious technical scope. Each poem uses a variety of metrical forms and is divided into a number of sections. "Movement," however, would be a better word than "section"; for the change from long unrhymed descriptive lines to ballad quatrains to octosyllabic couplets to exultant Psalm-like passages has the effect of music—the reader may be reminded of the balancing of recitative, aria, and chorus in an oratorio. The length of the poems helps Nicholson build an atmosphere which may create emotional acceptance for his subject, and the divisions serve partly to move the narrative forward and partly to reveal the central symbol from different angles.

The simplest of the poems is "The Bow in the Cloud," a lyrically ornamented version of the Flood story in Genesis vi–x. Section I relates the story to the contemporary, post-diluvian world which awaits not the Flood but the Second Coming—specifically, the shore off Hodbarrow Mines at sunset, which had been the setting of "By the Sea":

> The wooden groins run back from the shore
> To the long seawall that hoards in its rocky cordon
> The pitshafts with wheels like a sailor's helm,
> The rubble red and dark in the sandy dusk,
> The mines where once the purple ore was broken
> To boom as a gun or ring out as a clattering peal.

[54]

After a lively, Audenesque ballad in which Noah, in the form of "Old Tyson," a farmer and revivalist local preacher, takes aboard his quota of animals, Section III presents the Flood as a cosmic cataclysm. Nicholson is tempted into too "apocalyptic" a manner of writing, but the final lines—albeit echoing Eliot's "Gerontion"—convey powerfully the terror of the animal kingdom and mount to a fortissimo of final disintegration:

> And now the tall waves bound
> Over the mountain tops. The animals are drowned
> Where they crouch; the birds fly
> Till they drop. The sky
> Is black as a coal-pit, and the breaking moon
> Spreads in a belt of smoke and dusty rain,
> With a gravelly hail of flying shale
> Stretched behind like a comet's tail.
> It bursts as if charged with dynamite, is whirled
> In closing spirals, and the fragments hurled
> Down to the dark equator of the world.

The final section is tranquil, like the aftermath of a Lakeland thunderstorm. Tyson steps out on to Scafell Pike, the sun shines through "simmering mists," and God's covenant with man, the rainbow, is seen in the sky. The last lines of the poem foreshadow the endings of *The Old Man of the Mountains* and *Birth by Drowning;* with a typically Nicholsonian sense of proportion, Tyson returns to the duties and necessities of everyday life:

> The moon hangs in the bright sky,
> The bow fades in the cloud, the mist
> Rises like thanksgiving, the sea returns to its routine,
> And Tyson buckles his horse to the shafts of the plough.

Nicholson's impressive, musical handling of his material in this long poem and the simple moving eloquence of its last section require no doctrinal acceptance for appreciation. The vitality and imaginativeness of the language involve the reader almost physically in Nicholson's vivid re-creation of Noah's flood.

"The Holy Mountain" is much less successful. The first and last sections juxtapose the Garden of Eden, seen in terms of an idyllic

Cumberland valley, with the vision of a heaven based on Isaiah xi:9, in which the post-lapsarian miseries of man and of the animal kingdom will finally be removed and "the earth shall be full of the knowledge of the Lord/ As the waters cover the sea." The verse form of the last section recalls Christopher Smart's "Jubilate Agno," and its prophetic language has something of the homeliness, as well as the force, of Old Testament simile: "The earth shall be crushed like an olive for the sacred oil,/ Fermented like the grape, ground like corn in the mill,/ And burned like lard." The Cumberland landscape of the Garden of Eden in Section I is described with a different kind of eloquence; lyrical rhythm and loving descriptive particularity combine to elevate the catalogue of flowers and trees into a poetry of the factual:

The orchard grows on the slope that slants to the sun—
Damson, bullace and crab, and gean, the wild cherry,
White as lambs in spring. And the flowers of the dale,
Bigger than those of the fells, frailer than those of the fields:
The globe-flower, like a lemon, quartered but unpeeled;
The bell-flower, hanging its blue chime from a steeple of nettle-leaves,
Betony and cow-wheat, golden-rod and touch-me-not,
And in the woods, enchanter's nightshade,
And by the river, daffodils.

It is possible to respond directly to both these sections. The difficulty lies in the two middle sections which explain man's fallen state by means of two rival theories set forth in N. P. Williams's book *The Ideas of the Fall and Original Sin* (1927). Section III of the poem deals with the usual Fall story as told in Genesis iii, but from the point of view not of man but of the Apple of Knowledge, whose swelling and rotting symbolizes human pride; the section is overlaid with too much detail and goes on far too long. Section II deals with the Fall of the Rebel Angels, an unfamiliar story recounted in The Book of Enoch, without some knowledge of which Nicholson's references to "the Watchers" and "the four rivers" are quite obscure. Again, the section continues too long and allows Nicholson to indulge, according to a hostile review in *Scrutiny,* "a persistent interest in apocalyptic events and fantasies."[14] Certainly the running together of different accounts of the Fall stems from an interest in theological speculation and from a knowledge of esoteric biblical writings which even the Christian reader cannot be expected to share.

"The Garden of the Innocent" is the shortest of the three poems, and its reliance on biblical materials is comparatively slight: the Eden which it describes is less the one of Genesis than one of moral innocence which animals inhabit but from which fallen man is excluded. A poem about Original Sin, its approach may be called philosophical or existential; unlike the other two (referred to by one reviewer as being only "the impersonal organisation of scriptural story"[15]), this poem invites the reader's participation by its introspective use of the first person and by its Kafka-like sense of the human predicament. Section II describes man's search for innocence in his own subconscious, but man soon realizes that he will not discover it in the jungle of fear and animal instincts which the subconscious seems to be:

> The darkness skulks in crevices;
> A rabbit squeals at a stoat's eyes.
> Where the spruce bends like a green claw
> The furry silence slinks away.
> The fir trees scream like knife on bone,
> The sap like blood pounds through the pine.

Section III, portentously echoing T. S. Eliot, celebrates the amoral innocence of the animals whom, at this stage, man envies:

For these there are no bounds to the garden, neither inside nor outside,
Those who do not hear the voice, and, without hearing, obey.
They do not choose whether to know or know not,
Neither choose rightly nor choose wrongly.
They do not know what it is to choose or choose not.
They know neither temptation nor conscience, choose neither
    innocence nor sin.

The fourth section is a rather obscure ballad, its mountain-climbing narrative recalling Auden and Isherwood's *The Ascent of F6,* which seems to be a parable of man's search for forbidden knowledge which led to the Fall. The last section comes to terms with the imperfect human state; man is what he is and must make the best of it. The animals are now not only (as in Section I) "the creatures who have never been me" but "the creatures whom I can never be." The poem's final lines, with a bleakness reminiscent of Eliot's verse in parts of

Murder in the Cathedral, indicate that man's life must be lived on the terms laid down at the end of Genesis iii. Even such a life, however, possesses dignity and the possibility of development:

> That to which we cannot return is not to be found before us;
> There is no other garden beyond the bright sea.
> The nettle will follow the opportune harrow,
> The thorn increase in the blandishments of spring.
> Not in the prospectus of a blind tomorrow,
> But in the scything of nettles shall we find bread,
> In the burning of thorns shall we find warmth.
> The hand that is stung by nettles shall know deftness,
> The foot that is pricked by thorns shall develop strength.

The language of "The Garden of the Innocent" is sometimes stilted, rhetorical, and derivative (the opening of Section V closely resembles Kathleen Raine's poem "The Crystal Skull," for instance); but Nicholson's attempt to use biblical myth as the basis for a psychological study of man's nature and his place in the world is still impressive. Even if the reader accepts Eliot's view[16] that the bid for major stature of all three long poems did not succeed, he may still feel that "The Garden of the Innocent," in aiming at something more difficult than the other two, is the most praiseworthy failure.

Nicholson's biblical poems form a thematic group peculiar to *Five Rivers,* and they indicate his concern at this stage with direct representation of his Christian beliefs. They spring quite naturally from his declaration made in 1940 that "it is time that I trained my tongue to speak of God." It is possible, however, that a reviewer's comment on *Selected Poems* (1943), in which "The Garden of the Innocent" and "The Holy Mountain" first appeared, to the effect that "part of Nicholson's fascination is that he exacts not even a temporary belief from the unbeliever,"[17] may have stuck in his mind and suggested to him the obstacles to wide communication set up by his overtly Christian approach. At any rate, after *Five Rivers* a bifurcation occurred in his work: he continued to treat religious themes, but he did so in verse plays where their individual human relevance could emerge more fully. In his poems, he concentrated on landscape and man's relationship to it in such a way that these subjects could be seen to have religious significance yet retain the reader's interest for their own sake.

In this connection, the most significant poem in *Five Rivers* is the

[58]

very fine "To the River Duddon." Not only does its confident handling
of rangy, unrhymed lines show a far greater technical maturity than the
pleasant jog-trot of "Five Rivers" (to which its title might at first seem
to attach it as a mere appendix), but its search for a meaning in
landscape goes much deeper than the title poem's colorful but random
catalogue of local attractions. "To the River Duddon" contains a
description of the Duddon's course from near Wrynose Pass to where it
flows into the estuary on which Nicholson's home town of Millom
stands. The fact that the Duddon is Nicholson's "home river" explains
why he addresses it directly, and the use of the first person (which
distinguishes this poem from the other local poems in the volume)
indicates the degree of his involvement. The description is framed by
two attitudes to Wordsworth: the first, a satirical view of the rather
pedestrian Wordsworth revealed in the *Duddon Sonnets*; the second, a
respectful picture of "the old man, inarticulate and humble," from
whom the modern Cumbrian poet realizes he can learn. The poem
therefore not only describes a river but presents a train of thought.

In the second of his *Duddon Sonnets* Wordsworth bardically
apostrophized the river: "Child of the clouds! Remote from every
taint/ Of sordid industry thy lot is cast." Nicholson, after quoting part
of this, comments pungently: "But you and I know better, Duddon
lass." Nicholson's condensation of Wordsworth's thirty-four sonnets
into an unbroken thirty-two-line verse sentence which follows all the
changes, twists and turns, of the river is made in a similarly ironic spirit:
the images are slightly comic, a deliberate deflation of Wordsworth's
elevated diction. Yet their vigor and accuracy display no less love for
the Duddon than the older poet had felt:

> Past Cockley Beck Farm and on to Birks Bridge,
> Where the rocks stride about like legs in armour,
> And the steel birches buckle and bounce in the wind
> With a crinkle of silver foil in the crisp of the leaves;
> On then to Seathwaite, where like a steam-navvy
> You shovel and slash your way through the gorge
> By Wallabarrow Crag, broader now
> From becks that flow out of black upland tarns
> Or ooze through golden saxifrage and the roots of rowans;
> Next Ulpha, where a stone dropped from the bridge
> Swims like a tadpole down thirty feet of water
> Between steep skirting-boards of rock.

Nicholson eventually comes to realize that Wordsworth was more than "a middle-aged Rydal landlord/ With a doting sister and a pension on the Civil List"; he was more than a poet in retirement who wrote sonnets intended as a guidebook, on which Nicholson's description is a mock attack. Beneath the changing appearance of landscape Wordsworth was able to see an underlying permanence—he "knew that eternity flows in a mountain beck." In a broadcast in 1952, Nicholson made quite clear the nature of his admiration for Wordsworth: "It was not the beauty of nature which was Wordsworth's prime concern—not the beauty but the fact, not the spectacle but the objective reality behind the spectacle. . . . He loved his lakes and mountains not just for what they looked like, but for what they were. . . . Wordsworth's mountains were always real mountains."[18]

On this reality, Nicholson's own poems were increasingly to concentrate. By the intensity of his concentration he is able to make plain not only his own love for his region but his belief that "Christianity is one of the most materialist of religions. It holds that matter matters."[19] For Nicholson the basic "matter" of the created world is rock. That rock, while still itself, is also a natural symbol for the permanence of God. The magnificent peroration of "To the River Duddon" allies Nicholson with Wordsworth, and drives down like a drill to the fundamental rock which, geologically, is Nicholson's frequent subject and, metaphorically, his characteristic way of expressing his love of the created world and his belief in its Creator:

He knew beneath mutation of year and season,
Flood and drought, frost and fire and thunder,
The frothy blossom on the rowan and the reddening of the berries,
The silt, the sand, the slagbanks and the shingle,
And the wild catastrophes of the breaking mountains,
There stands the base and root of the living rock,
Thirty thousand feet of solid Cumberland.

The publication of *Five Rivers* established Nicholson's reputation as a poet to be taken seriously. It was widely, and on the whole warmly, reviewed. John Betjeman called Nicholson "a real poet";[20] Julian Symons called him "a considerable poet" and spoke of his "brilliant and original talent."[21] The volume was also successful with the public: a second impression was produced in August, 1944, and a third in September, 1945. Its success may partly be explained by reference to the renewed interest in poetry which prevailed during the war, but the qualities of Nicholson's poetry itself provide deeper answers. It is forthright, technically stimulating, and vivid in language; and it shows evidence of the sort of imaginative power which was probably welcome to people imprisoned by the realities, harsh or humdrum, of wartime. Nicholson's *persona,* that of an Orwellian "decent" man whose experiences are not remote from those of his ordinary readers, is an appealing one; and it seems likely that his Christianity, whatever barriers it may have set up to full critical recognition, provided a link between him and many of his readers in the wartime period in which his first volume appeared.

Five Rivers is not without its faults. Very often Nicholson's lively imagination dissipates itself in mere flights of exaggerated fancy; frequently words seem to beget words; images, images. A poem is sometimes betrayed by the desire for a local effect which, though piquant, is infelicitous in the total context; an instance of this occurs in "Stalingrad: 1942," where the comparison of "broken sandstone slabs" to "gingerbread" lowers the would-be heroic tone. "Now in the Time of this Mortal Life" is marred by the excruciating homophonic pun "By raising raisins unto blood," and in "September in Shropshire" Nicholson reveals a tendency to see objects too patly in terms of decorative metaphor, when he speaks of "the blue/ Earrings of bilberries in the tiny lobes of the leaves."

That a relatively young poet's first collection should contain flawed work is quite to be expected, and Nicholson's mistakes are generally due to an excess of verbal inventiveness, itself a quality without which poems would hardly be written. But *Five Rivers* has one special positive quality which is largely missing from Nicholson's later volumes—a quality which can only be described, lamely, as "magic." This "magic" seems most obviously to operate in poems in which Nicholson is registering the Celtic atmosphere that, like the Norse (celebrated with appropriate vigor in "For the Grieg Centenary"), is part of the heritage of Cumberland. It emerges briefly in the last lines of "Five Rivers," already quoted, and it is shown most extensively in the sequence "Songs of the Island." These three poems reveal a very sensitive balancing of rhyme and half-rhyme and, in their rhythms, an effect of ebb-and-flow which, taken together, enhance the incantatory suggestiveness of the words themselves:

Daily I watch the ships
Topple beyond the horizon where the sunset dips,
Daily I hear the sea whisper with wet lips.

The ships sail to the island and never come back,
Only a broken barrel drifts against the rock,
Only a spar or sailor's fingers tangled in the wrack.

Daily at the shingle's edge I gather wood,
And pick the sea-coal from bladders of salty weed,
Daily I feel the tug of the tide in my blood.

                                        ("Maiden's Song")

This quality of Romantic lyricism is also found in more distinctively personal poems like "Coastal Journey," where the ordinary activity of riding a train from Barrow-in-Furness to Millom gives rise to a haunting sense of timelessness. In the meditative "Askam Unvisited," long fluent lines quietly follow the weavings of the poet's thoughts and deftly create for those thoughts a rich local atmosphere. Such poems as these suggest a sensitive mind well able to communicate its perceptions. Nicholson's later poems—more muscular in their rhythms, more tightly structured, and more conscious of having definite ideas to transmit—are perhaps more wholly satisfying, and they are certainly poems which only Nicholson could have written; but they lack the element of magic and the particular kind of sensitivity that are among the most pleasing features of Nicholson's first volume.

II   Rock Face

Nicholson's second collection, *Rock Face,* was published in 1948. The solidity suggested by its title, however, is largely illusory: the title poem itself is short and almost inconsequential, and the volume as a whole displays a diffuseness of purpose which prompts the label "transitional." Reviewers confined their praise to only a few of its forty poems,[22] and to see *Rock Face* in meaningful relation to the volumes which precede and follow it involves a comparable singling-out. Such highly selective discussion does less of an injustice to the poems left out than might at first appear. A characteristic of *Rock Face* is that many poems in it seem to spring from purely random impulses, unlinked either to any intellectual content or to any particular prompting "occasion." There seems, simply, to be a shortage of subject matter. A quarter of the poems in the volume use the word "song" in their titles; though some, like "Snow Song," are pleasant and limpid, others, like "A Second Song at Night," merely strike rhetorical attitudes. The essential point about all of them is that they could easily have been written by someone else. The sense they give of a person speaking is deceptive; what they really reveal is a poet too conscious that he is writing poetry.

Support for such a view is given by "The Candle," the unique example in Nicholson's work of a poem about poetry. Its first line, and the imagery of its first section, were suggested to him by Kathleen Raine:

> Poetry is not an end.
> The flame is where the candle turns
> To smoke, solid to air,
> Life to death, or say,
> To that which still is life in another way.
> The flame is not an aim,
> Nor the brightest light
> Any justification for its burning.

The initial statement is a pretty accurate description of Nicholson's usual attitude to poetry, for what he seems to be asserting is a hostility to any "art-for-art's-sake" view of it. But when in the second section the idea is elaborated in terms of the non-equivalence of "love" and "the beloved," what emerges is a vague search for the abstraction "poetry" as something apart from the created poem. The final lines suggest that the writing of poetry is a process of self-discovery:

> The flame is the poem,
> And the light shines little time,
> And the poet follows the rhyme into the darkness
> And learns there his new unspoken name.

Interest in the possible truth of Nicholson's theorizing is reduced by the fragmentariness of the poem itself. Whereas the influence of Kathleen Raine's thought can be positively felt in the volume as a whole in Nicholson's concern with an image as fundamental as that of rock, in this poem the influence of her rather abstract style has the effect of turning him away from his more frequent concern with poetry as a way of expressing in words the objective world which the eye perceives. What may be called the "transcendental method" of Kathleen Raine does not come naturally to Nicholson.

A better poem than "The Candle" is "St. Luke's Summer" in which an adroit selection of images from the visual world enables Nicholson to establish a relationship between the declension of autumn and the hibernation of the poetic faculty. This poem cannot be called just a poem about poetry; for, though the last lines state that ". . . while dead leaves clog the eyes/ Never-predicted poetry is sown," this conclusion seems to grow out of the description of natural processes which has preceded it. This description can be enjoyed for its own sake, without the suspicion that a moral is being forced. The poet's consciousness of his calling is subsumed in the man's loving reaction to the world around him, and the equivalence of sound and sense in the fourth line of the second stanza is particularly admirable:

> Beside the trellis of the bowling green
> The poppy shakes its pepper-box of seed;
> Groundsel feathers flutter down;
> Roses exhausted by the thrust of summer
> Lose grip and fall; the wire is twined with weed.

The last lines, quoted earlier, of "St. Luke's Summer" can be taken without strain on three levels: Nicholson is talking about the poetic process, the way in which the subconscious assimilates experiences even though the "fancy" seems "run to seed and dry as stone"; at the same time, under the surface of "brown October days" the natural world is also moving to spring; and the final image of "sowing" has religious overtones, suggesting that the birth of poetry and the rebirth of nature are both part of a larger pattern. The image, broadly, is one of resurrection. Endings of this type are found in quite a number of poems in *Rock Face*—in "Autumn," "Early March," "To a Child before Birth," "The Crocus," and even, though with a slightly different slant, in "A Street in Cumberland" and in the title poem itself.

This prevalence of religious undertones is symptomatic of a striking difference between *Rock Face* and *Five Rivers* which leads the reader to take the word "transitional" less in its negative implication of unsettledness of style and content and more in its positive suggestion of poems moving toward a new kind of expression. The difference was neatly indicated in a review of *Rock Face* by Howard Sergeant: "...Nicholson is now giving far less attention to the superficial aspects and more to the intrinsic values of Christianity... his material is better assimilated.... As a result, his work not only shows a greater depth of thought and imaginative quality, but is more authentic in expressing the Christian interpretation of life through his own poetic experience."[23]

Nicholson's final view of man in "The Garden of the Innocent" was that he was a fallen creature who had to live within the limits imposed by his fallen state. This fallen state is the subject of "Across the Estuary," a poem which is religious in the sense put forward by Howard Sergeant: it renders a Christian attitude in terms of Nicholson's "own poetic experience," instead of playing variations on a theme already laid down by biblical history or myth. "Across the Estuary" communicates its view of man precisely because its rendering of the natural landscape in which he is placed is so convincing in its own right. Nicholson adapts a piece of local history—the regular crossing of the Kent, Leven, and Duddon estuaries in earlier centuries—into an allegory of man's moral choices; but the estuary itself functions in the poem in three ways. It is real, and thus involves the reader physically in the careful steps which must be taken in order to cross it safely; it is the natural context in which man is tried and found wanting; and it is also symbolic of the moral choice itself, in that the firm sand of reason all too soon changes into the dangerous quicksand of uncertainty and mistake.

The poem is in four sections, but the fact that the meter of the first and last sections is the same underlines the basic sameness of setting and gives the poem a neat circularity of construction. Section 1 appears at first to be pure description of the estuary at the turn of the tide:

> Here, under the canvas of the fog,
> Is only sand, and the dead, purple turf,
> And gulleys in the mud where now the water
> Thrusts flabby fingers. The wild geese
> Feed beneath the mist, grey and still as sheep,
> And cormorants curl black question-marks
> Above the threshold of the sea.

But the image of fog, and the absence from view of either bank of the estuary, have a sinister quality which the "question-mark" metaphor seems designed to emphasize, and with the phrase "here is the track," the reader becomes clearly aware, because of the human being whose presence is implied, of the dangers of the scene. It is his predicament which the initial description is designed to highlight. His steps miss the marked track, and the lines that show his trying to find it again have the same immediacy evident in the prewar poem "No Man's Land":

> But now—where is the track? Where are the ruts? The broom
> Skulks back into the dark, and every footstep,
> Dug deep in mud, draws water through the heels.
> Each step goes wrong. Here, forward—deep, the sand
> Shifts under foot like scree. Backward—deeper.
> Stand still then—squids of sand
> Wrap suckers round my feet.

The section ends with the traveler stranded by the rising tide.

Section II supplies a key to the foregoing description: it is not merely a historical exercise but has a contemporary moral significance. Section III takes the reader inside the traveler's mind, and the use of the first person implicates both poet and reader in his predicament. The turning aside from the marked track is now seen to symbolize man's mistaken choices contingent on his fallen state. Though the causes of his moral dilemma lie in the past, and though "the past is forgiven," each man carries in himself a moral obligation in the present which, because of Original Sin, he is unable completely to fulfill: "It is not then but now/ That tightens like mist about me:/ Not how I came/ But where I am,/ Not what I was,/ Nor how I grew/ From that to this,/ But merely/ My being I."

This discussion states more overtly than the poem itself the Christian meaning of the third section. Nicholson himself, in bare lines which suggest the stripping off in time of trial of the protecting layers of human personality, wisely refrains from using obviously Christian images; and the reader, if he wishes, may see the section simply as the instant recapitulation of the individual life said to accompany drowning, or as man's sense of guilt or inadequacy to which he cannot assign a specific cause. The last section returns to the physical scene, but this time all is covered by the tide and "There is no sign of traveller on the flat waters." It is a world in which "The inevasible choice of wrong and less wrong/ Is forgotten or deferred." This ambiguous phrase allows the reader to take the end of the poem as a picture of either a post-human world or of the non-human world before the Fall.

In "Across the Estuary" Nicholson makes very effective use of his local background, both historically and pictorially; but the poem cannot be called primarily a regional one, and its relevance is not even physically limited to the landscape it describes. One of the biggest surprises in *Rock Face*, if it is read after *Five Rivers*, is the complete absence from it of regional poems, or at least of the kind of regional poems so frequent in the earlier volume: poems which attempt to capture the essence of a particular place, either by visual sketching or by the listing of significant historical details.

"Thomas Gray in Patterdale" suggests an explanation for Nicholson's change in emphasis. The poem begins by describing a Lakeland landscape—Helvellyn seen from the southern end of Ullswater—as Thomas Gray would have seen it through the falsifying medium of a Claude-glass.[24] Such a view is too smooth, too artistically neat; and Gray is finally shown as becoming aware of its incompleteness. He realizes that he himself is "part of a landscape that I cannot view." The "picturesque" attitude places man in too arrogant a relationship to the world, a relationship which implies self-deception. The breathlessness of the poem's last lines conveys a wish to break the pose of aloofness and a sense that man, too, belongs to the world of nature:

> What if I listen? What if I learn?
> What if I break the glass and turn
> And face the objective lake and see
> The wide-eyed stranger skyline look at me?

Gray in this poem is certainly a surrogate for Nicholson himself, and the idea that man is as much observed as observer may well explain the impersonality of the poems now to be discussed. These poems, when they present man at all, present him in terms of natural objects or as involved in natural processes. A quotation from one of Nicholson's radio talks helps to explain why these poems attempt, not to capture the spirit of place by pictorial composition in words, but to look beneath the surface to the bare bones so starkly revealed in the last line of "To the River Duddon": " 'View' is a term I do not like. A view is something which takes place in the eye, in the brain. It is an accident, created merely by the position in which the beholder happens to be, merely by the geometrical relationship between the eye and a number of external objects. And I would rather tell you about the rocks which made up that view. For all of it could be explained in terms of the rocks, and of the forces which had worked on them."[25]

The total impression made by Nicholson's second volume certainly differs from that created by the strong local tang of *Five Rivers.* Kathleen Raine, reading the poems before publication, put forward "Rock Face" as a suitable title for them. Such a title evokes a monolithic expanse like a cliff, at any rate something large and elemental; but the poem which Kathleen Raine's title provoked Nicholson to write rather punctures this expectation. The face referred to resembles a human face which Nicholson sees in the exposed side of a quarry:

> . . .brow and nose and eyes
> Cleft in a stare of ten-year old surprise,
> With slate lids slid backward, grass and plantain
> Tufted in ear and nostril, and an ooze
> Like drip from marble mouth that spews
> Into the carved trough of a city fountain.

There is a little more to the poem, however, than this somewhat whimsical anthropomorphizing of nature. The rock of the quarry is later carted away to be used as building material, and what interests Nicholson is the way in which, distortedly, the lineaments of the original rock can still be traced in the object which man makes of it: "The rock face, temple, mouth and all,/ Peers bleakly at me from this dry-stone wall."[26] "Rock Face" already shows Nicholson's sense of the strong link which exists for him between man and his environment, but the actual tone of the poem is one of understatement; the movement from rock face in quarry to rock face in wall has almost the effect of a conceit, and the quietness with which the poem's point is made is greatly akin to the reticent wit of Andrew Young, whose poem "The Haystack" displays a similarity of idea and phrasing.[27]

Somewhat similar to "Rock Face" in its idea is "A Street in Cumberland," which describes the way in which the past, in the shape of a two hundred-year-old farm—itself built of quarried rock—survives visibly into the present even though "the rest of the street was shunted firm/ Against it when the town was built on the mosses." Here again the continuity of rock attracts Nicholson's imagination. The farm, which stands in a street in Millom just round the corner from the poet's home, yearns back even beyond its earlier days of isolation to the time when it was unquarried:

> Yet a dream
> Grips at the house when the roofs are asleep,
> True to the loins of the rock that bred it. When the slag
> Is puddled across the clouds, and curlews fly
> Above the chimneys, the walls thrust like a crag
> Through the dark tide of haematite in the night sky.

Technically the poem is something of an oddity. It starts in a quite neat iambic rhythm, but later on certain of the factual details refuse to accommodate themselves to the rhythm, and the resulting effect jars: "Come round to the back and you will find/ The old uncovered walls—slate bosses/ Two foot by two, with cobble-ducks for gable-end." Similarly, though an *abab* quatrain rhyme scheme is used throughout, the sentences continually run beyond the line endings, as though bursting out of badly fitting clothes. The total impression is of an attempt to use speech rhythms, but also of a lack of the confidence that would allow them to form their own metrical patterns.

Images of winter occur again and again in *Rock Face,* sharpening the effect of bleakness which prompted a number of reviewers to compare Nicholson to the composer Jean Sibelius. The bleakest poem in the volume is "The Land Under the Ice," which describes the coming of the Ice Age to Cumberland and the shaping of the landscape into its present form. Kathleen Raine called it "a kind of winter Georgic,"[28] but the description is misleading. The "Statesman," who is the only "human" figure in the poem, is not a realistic Cumbrian farmer but a sort of Methusaleh who survives the "ten thousand years" of the Ice Age and who in Section III returns to "a landscape unfamiliar, yet his own." He seems to represent Man (as a creature dependent on Nature), but he is far more an abstraction than a human being. His final invocation, smacking distinctly of such Roy Campbell poems as "The Albatross," has a rhetorical nobility rather than any personal warmth:

> O in the white night of the bone I've heard
> The senile north gods howling long and high;
> The wind-god, shrieking like a migrant bird
> That drills the carbon blackness of the sky.

In that it follows the sequence of the geological process which is its subject matter, the poem has a rudimentary narrative line; but it does not seem to develop any idea, and its use of rather static quatrains tends to turn it into a series of set pieces. Individual lines and stanzas display descriptive sharpness and an inventive use of metaphor, but the intrinsic impersonality of the subject precludes imaginative involvement in the poem as a whole. A stanza like the following is symptomatic of its rather archaic style:

> The Statesman from the dalehead herds the sheep,
> Gimmer and lambs, to summer heaf;
> And when the scraggy oats are ripe,
> By walls of purple cobble piles the sheaf.

The technical dialect words for "young ewe" and "fell-pasture," and even the tart colloquialism "scraggy," are unable to overcome the rather stiff inversions and the Augustan pastoral style of the last line. The old-fashioned language and the rigid stanza form may be intended as an apt reflection of the distance in time of the Ice Age; but, if so, they do not succeed. When Nicholson three years later deals with geological raw material in "The Seven Rocks," his free and varied mode of presentation persuades the reader of the human relevance of what is presented. In "The Land Under the Ice," poetic diction only underlines thematic remoteness.

The last poem in *Rock Face,* "Silecroft Shore," is able to enlist the reader's partial sympathy because it is a meditation rather than a narrative. The reader is aware of a man thinking and of the strong current of feeling which exists between the poet and the natural objects he contemplates. Kathleen Raine identified very sensitively the reaction the poem produces: ". . . one senses that Norman Nicholson often feels himself to be a living particle of the natural world, a kind of mysticism of the bones."

The poem is in five sections. The shore at Silecroft faces the Irish Sea, some four miles from Millom; and the incident from which the poem originates is presented in Section II. The poet, walking along the shingly shore, picks up a pebble whose appearance and history he describes with minute particularity:

> An indigo mud-stone, from Skiddaw or Black Combe,
> Snapped off the rocks and carried to the sea

In the pockets of the ice, its sides planed flat
To long unequal rhomboids; then
Shaken daily in the dice-box of the surf,
Hammered, filed and sandpapered, its roughnesses are rounded,
And what was once a chip, a sliver of slate,
Becomes a whole, self-axelled and self-bounded,
Grained like a bird's egg and simple as a raindrop,
A molecule of beauty.

It is not difficult to see that the pebble's development has a human relevance: the pebble is like an individual, born of a larger body (society or parent) and molded by environment and experience until he too acknowledges "no way/ Other of being than this."

The reader is quietly persuaded into accepting the pebble on the symbolic as well as the literal level by the poem's first section, which in hypnotic two-stress lines rings the changes on the poem's two basic terms, *stone* and *bone:* "Stone is the earth's/ Cool skeleton,/ And bone the rock/ That flesh builds on." Sections III and IV follow naturally from this premise that man is connected to the earth on which he lives, and they describe geological processes—erosion, fossilization, petrifaction—anthropomorphically through metaphor. Section IV also contributes a lyrical interlude to the musical structure of the poem as a whole.

The last section returns to the introspective mood and to the rocking rhythm of the first, but it develops the idea of memory which had been implicit in the previous sections. The poet's interest in natural processes is more than an academic one: it is as if, in observing rock and stone, he has been harking back to an earlier existence of himself, as if he were now the farthest point of an evolutionary progression that began with rock, with which he still feels a sense of kinship. Man is in himself the sum of natural history, and his memories and dreams reach back into the remote geological past: "Memory flows/ Cool round the bone,/ ... And the bone says:/ 'It is not I/ That bears the daisy head/ But the limestone generations of the dead." The end of the poem abandons logic, allegory and symbolism in favor of a yearning that is almost mystical. A "poem about geology" has become, it seems, a religious nostalgia for some lost Eden:

> Oh! cobble on the shore
> Can you not remember

> What you were before
> The valleys were brought low?
> Can you not forget
> What it is to never know
> Rock turning slowly
> Back into rock
> Long to-days ago?

Strangely moving as these lines are, they reveal a sensibility unlikely to be shared by very many readers. The underlying theme of much of *Rock Face*—that rock is the skeleton on which not only the earth but human life is built—may well strike a reader as the kind of truth which is so fundamental that its bare expression seems irrelevant to life as man lives it from day to day. It must be admitted that, whatever the merits of individual poems, there is a certain monotony about *Rock Face* as a whole.[29] It may perhaps be said that, in eschewing the surface regionalism and explicitly religious themes of *Five Rivers,* Nicholson has dug if anything too deeply into the "thirty thousand feet of solid Cumberland." Giles Romilly, though he made it crudely, made a true point when he said in a review of *Rock Face* that "If Mr. Nicholson would . . . dry off *some part* of the estuary mud and the river-bed slime, and venture for once *towards* a built-up area, I believe that there might be cause to be glad."[30] In discovering, in his third volume, the poetic potential of his home town of Millom, Nicholson was to do exactly what Romilly suggested.

III   The Pot Geranium

Nicholson's third and most important volume, *The Pot Geranium,* appeared in 1954. It was the first collection of poems to be recommended by the newly formed Poetry Book Society to its members. The short poem "On my Thirty-Fifth Birthday" (1949) furnishes a rare insight into Nicholson's mind at the time the collection was taking shape, and it also gives a number of clues about the sort of poem he was interested in writing. Three quotations illustrate how apt it is as a comment on *The Pot Geranium.* Nicholson first asserts that "There is no time for words/ Unless the words have meaning; no time for poetry,/ Unless the poem has a purpose." The broad truth of Nicholson's assertion about his poetry's need for a purpose is borne out by the way in which many of the poems in his third volume do seem concerned with making a point, either about life in general or about the particular slant on life obtained by living in a small town. The characteristic note of the volume is confidence, both of language and idea: the poems know where they are going, and the reader is aware in most cases of a solid intellectual structure beneath their surface.

In the second stanza of "On My Thirty-Fifth Birthday" Nicholson adds that "There is no time for love,/ But love of the world in the one." His treatment of Millom as a replica of society at large is closely linked with this idea. And the poem's conclusion, that there is "No time for time/ But only for eternity," can be read as explaining his emphasis not on what differentiates places but on what they have in common. It obviously indicates, also, the religious substratum of Nicholson's thinking, which enables him to see all places, all temporal phenomena, in relation to the eternal truths which, for him, give them their meaning and their purpose. Such an outlook was succinctly expressed in "On Being a Provincial," which develops overtly the conclusions already reached poetically in *The Pot Geranium:* ". . . in the geography of the timeless world, the world that does *not* change, all . . . places are equidistant from their true capital, and even the metropolis is no more than one of heaven's provincial towns."[3 1]

In 1949 Nicholson wrote at some length about the kind of imagery he uses. For him, images derive from "the world around me"—from external objects rather than from "subjective sources, from dreams, myths and the subconscious."[3 2] While not completely true of Nicholson's poetry before 1948, this statement is a broadly accurate indication of his direction after *Rock Face* and goes a long way towards explaining the vein of "commonsensicality" which characterizes his work from the end of the 1940s onwards. Having established the firm footing that his imagery has in the external world, he explains that, for him, an object has meaning in three ways": it means something simply as an object, shaped according to natural laws; it has a relationship to man; and it has an ultimate meaning which "contains all the others," its meaning to God, who created it. In Nicholson's poetry of this period all three "meanings"—natural, human, and religious—are present in varying degrees; but the one he chooses to emphasize, the one which is the imaginative center of most of the poems in *The Pot Geranium,* is the second, the human one.

This "human meaning" is most obviously found in "From Walney

Island," which is almost a demonstration of Nicholson's statements
about imagery. The poem shows in its own development the
transformation of a world which is at first merely seen and described
into a world which, when once the human element has been
appreciated, is felt and understood. The poem begins with a description
of the shipbuilding town of Barrow-in-Furness as it is observed from
Walney Island which lies opposite it:

> An oily fog
> Smudges the mud-mark till the screes of slag
> Seem floating on the water. Smoke and fog
> Wash over crane and derrick, and chimney stacks
> Ripple and ruck in the suck and swim of the air
> Like fossil trunks of trees in a drowned forest.
> Away in the docks the unlaunched hulls of ships
> Seem sunk already, lying on the swash bed
> With barnacles and algae.

The impressionism of this passage seems at first to be explicable as a
visual distortion promoted by the "smoke and fog," but the second
section presents it as the effect of the uncontrolled workings of the
"fancy" which "flashes about an abstract/ Underwater world of shapes
and shadows,/ Where men are only movement, where fire and furnace/
Are only highlights, lines and angles." The word "only" reveals the
poet's judgment on the picture which his fancy creates, and the reader
realizes that the scene has been set up in order to be demolished by the
latter half of the poem. As the tide ebbs, the poet notices "A dripping
rib of concrete, half bridge, half causeway,/ With neither curb nor
handrail,/ A foot above the water." Just as the presence of a human
being gives scale to a photograph of mountains, so this object suddenly
makes sense of the landscape in which it occurs. It becomes an image of
man which unlocks the emotional response, the sense of relevance,
which the poet's "insulated eye" has been unable to find in the
previously "private landscape":

> And like a stone
> Thrown through a window pane, the path
> Smashes the panorama, pricking the pattern, bringing back
> A human meaning to the scene. Shadows
> Are walls again, angles revert to roofs,

And roofs and walls relate themselves to men.
The hunger of a hundred thousand lives
Aches into brick and iron, the pain
Of generations in continual childbirth
Throbs through the squirming smoke, and love and need
Run molten into the cold moulds of time.

The combination of simple language and strong feeling makes a significant contrast to the poem's early elaboration of sight and sound patterns, and even the final line derives its justification not from a wish to create a memorable metaphorical conclusion but from the solid reality of the steelworks at Barrow-in-Furness which provides its image.

It was not, however, this poem (first published in July, 1951) which Nicholson had in mind when writing "The Image in my Poetry" but his long poem "The Seven Rocks." This poem is printed at the end of the volume, but it was in fact written by 1948, and first published in Cyril Connolly's influential magazine *Horizon* in December of that year. Next to "The Holy Mountain," "The Seven Rocks" is Nicholson's longest poem; and, in the sense that its subject is very unusual, it may reasonably be thought of as his most ambitious one. As one reviewer has noted ". . .poets of nature are common, but poets of geology are rare indeed."[33] But were "The Seven Rocks" only a geological descriptive piece, its relevance would be very limited. Only a poet interested in scientific fact could have written it, but for Nicholson there is no essential division between science and poetry: "Science, in fact, instead of destroying my conception of the world enriches and clarifies it, and it is when I have turned to science to help me understand the world around me that I have found much of the material for my poetry."[34]

"The Seven Rocks" functions on the literal level as a description of the main groups of rocks in the Lake District, but it is also an allegory for the Seven Cardinal Virtues of Christianity. For Nicholson, at least, there is nothing forced about his parallels—over many years spent in observing the mountains of his home area, he had come to think of their rocks in something like human terms. As one example, in Section III of the poem ("Coniston Flag"), Nicholson mentions "Kirkby Roundheads"—a kind of roofing slate found in the Furness area of North Lancashire. The overtone of charity here is not difficult to perceive; but should it be, Nicholson once made it explicit: "There is for me an inevitable connection between human charity and the rocks that give shelter in the form of roofing slate."[3 5] It would be a mistake to see the rocks of the poem merely as symbols, with no life of their own; but it would be equally mistaken to see the poem as no more than a versified geological survey.

The poem not only presents the rocks "in the order of their geological antiquity," starting at the Ordovician and ending with the Permian, but it also moves gradually through the seasons of the year, from winter to autumn. This overall design helps the reader to grasp the passing of time not just as a geological abstraction to be apprehended intellectually but in terms that can be related more immediately to human experience. The double pattern links together the cyclical processes of the contemporary visible world and the immensely longer, constantly repeated processes of stratification, volcanic explosion, and denudation which have created through millennia the landscape's present shape. The poem's final section completes the picture of geological and seasonal time by relating it to the human dimension which gives the poem its real relevance. Its autumn setting calls up thoughts of human life, decay, and death—and makes a second reading of the poem a more meaningful experience than the first.

Section I starts with a snow landscape, and this device produces both a feeling of gravity and an air of suspense which are underlined by the context of evening and by the slow, iambic-based lines:

> Night falls white as lime; the sky,
> Floury with cloud, reflects the rising glow
> Of the cumulus of earth. Only
> The seaward side of crags, the under-eaves
> Of trees, west-looking windows, gates and gables
> Unfrilled by snow, hold darkness still:
> Elsewhere the frost precipitates
> The once-dissolved, dry dregs of day.

The landscape with which Nicholson is concerned is that of Black Combe ("a humped white paradox"), the mountain which rises behind Millom; and his equation of the Skiddaw Slate of which it is composed with Faith is presumably made because the oldest rock is for him a fit symbol of the fundamental Christian virtue: "Here the river of time in a delta spread/ The bulged and buckled mud that heaves us firm/ As faith above the misty minutes." This section ends with a note of expectancy: just as the color white includes the whole spectrum of the rainbow, so winter is both the end of one year and the matrix out of which the variety of the next will emerge. The final image conveys a momentary stasis which holds within it the inevitability of future movement, of development and change: "The snow/ Holds the colour of the seasons/ Spinning into white, and time is frozen/ To a long, shining icicle of light."

With Section II, the icicle starts immediately to melt, not only in terms of the description itself, of time moving forward and the rocks emerging from beneath their covering of snow, but, with a musical sense of appropriateness, in the meter—short, nervous lines whose rhythm acts out what the words themselves say:

> The skin of the snow
> Breaks and wriggles
> From the napes of the fells
> Like white snakes;
> And blue as gentians
> The smooth crags shoot
> From green sepals
> Of grass and moss.

The three central sections are set in the context of spring. Section III is in octosyllabic couplets, and its subject is Coniston Flag, a stone used for paving slabs and for roofing slates. What Nicholson actually describes is a quarry, and its exposed strata are seen first as a museum of geological history. Quarries, for Nicholson, are a symbol of the connection between man and the landscape. From the rock come his houses, his roofs, and his walls; and, in this sense, as has been seen, the Coniston Flag rock is an appropriate image of charity:

> With Kirkby Roundheads on the roof
> Purple as polyanthus, proof
> Against the flocking, mid-March weather,
> When the wind's wing and the gull's feather
> Fly screaming off the sea together.

Section IV ("Eskdale Granite") uses the same meter as the first and last sections of the poem, and thus appears to form its central arch. A sense of rising is conveyed by the syntax which, by a three-fold repetition of the word *above* in the first sentence, seems to be striving upwards; and the comparison with fortitude, prompted by the bareness of the rock, gains force from the way in which the eye, slowly and with effort, is led higher and higher until it focuses on a fell top described as if it were a weatherbeaten human face. The expanded last line emphasizes the feeling of strength and achievement, the enduring quality of rock and, within his more limited time scale, of man:

> The eyes are hollow pots, the ears
> Clustered with carbuncles, and in the evening
> The warts of stone glow red as pencil ore
> Polished to a jewel, and the bronze brow wears
> Green fortitude like verdigris beneath a sleet of years.

Section V is in two parts, each describing an aspect of mountain limestone. The first presents it in terms of the "millions of sea-creatures" whose "skeletal remains"[36] comprise it. Nicholson shows the odd resemblance between limestone forms and shapes from the world of animate nature, thus suggesting a common pattern; for inherent in the static rock is the movement of prehistoric seas and the continuing growth of vegetation:

> Where flinty clints are scraped bone-bare
> A whale's ribs glint in the sun.
> Coral has built bright islands there,
> And birch and juniper fin the fell,
> Dark as a trawling under-wave. . .

In limestone, iron ore is found; and Nicholson moves in the second part of the section to Hodbarrow Point on the Duddon estuary and brings out explicitly the connection between the rock and the virtue of prudence which it symbolizes for him; it is seen as a hoarding by the "sea-beast bone" of a kind of "buried treasure," deposited throughout years of geological time. From the iron ore of Hodbarrow Mines sprang the Victorian prosperity of Millom, and Nicholson presents man's digging of the rock and his establishing of iron mines in imagery which suggests man's debt to nature and his likeness to estuary birds which dig with their beaks in the sand for food:

> Long-shank diviners stand
> Prodding and probing the land,

And steel nebs bore
Down to the hoard of ore;
The coffers of the rock
Spring open at the shock,
And a new life is built upon
The buried treasure of the bone.

The transition from "buried treasure" to the coal mining of Section VI ("Maryport Coal") is a straightforward one. Appropriately, the section is set in summer to convey both the warmth of the coal when it is used for fires and the semitropical climate which obtained during the Upper Carboniferous period when the coal measures were formed. Because the coal measures of Cumberland lie underneath much of what was once Inglewood Forest and because the outlaws of this forest were once celebrated in ballads, Nicholson has cast this section in the form of a Border ballad, which serves as an exuberant lyrical interlude beween the tight lines and stanzas of "Mountain Limestone" and the grave iambics of the poem's conclusion. Though the link betwcen this section and the virtue of justice seems tenuous and arbitrary, the myth-like presentation of coal as a buried sun which man digs up and turns again to fire is a plausibly fanciful way of showing how man draws his resources from nature:

They dragged deep in the fronded sea,
    Deep in the rocking land;
They hooked the sun at the ebb of the green
    And cast it on the sand.

And buds and bells and spikes of flame
    Flowered from the black bone's side;
And the seed of the sun burned back to the sun
    On the greenwood tide.

Throughout the first six sections of the poem, rock is described and a human interpretation is offered without the presence of the poet other than as an eye which observes. In the seventh and last section, "St. Bees Sandstone," Nicholson comes forward in the first person, as if to make quite clear the connection between the landscape and the man who sees it. As the poem began on a winter evening, it concludes on an evening in autumn, and the sole use of *I* in the second line makes the reader aware of the presence in the landscape of the human figure which gives the landscape scale and meaning. The poet's physical presence adds more feeling to the description, and the section reads as an elegiac meditation, a summing up. Autumn is an appropriate seasonal setting for the red of the sandstone, whose color recalls falling leaves; but autumn also gives the elegiac flavor; the gradual erosion of the sandstone is a natural symbol for the dying of the year and the death of the human individual:

> Across red slabs of rock
> I gaze down at the architectural sea. Now
> The same sea re-fingers back to sand
> That which was made from sand.
> . . . .
> Slowly the rock un-knows itself.

The word *un-knows* tacitly equates the process of rock erosion with the gradual dissolution of consciousness which accompanies ageing and dying, and it may also imply the change from one generation to another and one civilization to another. Life is a narrow "ribbon," and in the context of the inevitability of erosion

> Temperance is the one virtue.
>   To wait, accept,
> To let the wind blow over, and the sea
> Ebb and return, raise and destroy—that
> Is the one virtue.

Both rock and man are involved in an endlessly repeated cycle. As stratification and weathering are equally part of the geological process, so "only in life/ Can death define its purpose." The echo of the burial service, which concludes the poem and relates the decay of rock to that of man, implies no pessimistic finality. The poem's cyclical structure makes its last lines as much a fresh beginning as an ending:

> The sea
> Creeps up the sand and sandstone like a moss;
> The crest of the rocks is cracked like a breaking wave,
> The land declines again to its old rebirth:
> Ashes to ashes, sand to sand.

In displaying ability to deal with a number of levels of meaning simultaneously, in language which is dignified and moving without abandoning concreteness, Section VII of "The Seven Rocks" is one of Nicholson's finest pieces of writing. Indeed, the poem by and large is a remarkably successful example of his ability to communicate through regional material a universal significance. Certainly Nicholson's most effective long poem, it demonstrates a new-found freedom and muscularity of language, a felicity of imagery, and an over-all sense of musical structure which enables the reader to follow the main theme through all its "diversions"[37] and varying angles of approach. But, partly because of its sheer size, partly because it is the earliest of the poems included in *The Pot Geranium,* and partly because it places man in what is still, for most people, a context of inanimate nature, it is a poem which stands alone in the volume. In its last section's use of the first person, however, the reader may find a significant link with the poems most characteristic of the third volume—poems no less universal in their application but more personal in expression and intimately local in feeling.

Nicholson has never, in his poetry, been unaware of Cumberland as a whole, but what distinguishes *The Pot Geranium* from his other volumes is the special importance attached by the poems in it to his home town of Millom. While in *Five Rivers* and *Rock Face* Millom is certainly present as a context, it cannot quite be called the subject of a poem; and Nicholson's personal involvement with his birthplace is indicated only once when he refers to it, in "Askam Visited," as "the iron town which is my home." But, as Nicholson's poetry developed, so, it seems, did his interest in what was closest to him. It may be simply that, as his work became better known and favorably commented on, he grew more confident that his immediate environment would be of interest to people outside it. At any rate, he was able in 1952 to say that: "If a man wants to see things 'strange, rich and rare,' he should cross not to the other side of the world, but to the other side of his own street. Familiarity breeds blindness rather than contempt, and nothing has more power to surprise us than the familiar looked at for the first time."[38]

In dealing with Millom, Nicholson, instead of narrowing the relevance of his poems, paradoxically enlarges it. Although his presentation of Millom—its people, its houses, its speech—is very local in its concern for detail, the reader responds by feeling how much the

[81]

small town is a microcosm of the world. As Nicholson stated in his talk "On Being a Provincial": ". . .this preoccupation with what is local, this sense of belonging to a small, separate, ingrown, almost hermetically sealed community, has always been the experience of the vast majority. So that it is precisely here, in our intense concern with what is close to us, that we most resemble the people of other countries and other times. It is precisely here, rather than in any vague internationalism of outlook, that we can most readily sympathise with the rest of the world."

In fact, this awareness of and familiarity with his own town and area as a microcosm enable Nicholson to describe it in detail; for the universal conclusion justifies the "intense concern with what is close." A poem like "Ravenglass Railway Station" lists detail after local detail in the manner of "Five Rivers" but with greater clear-cut particularity; and at the end of the poem, the distinguishing marks of one particular place are drawn together in such a way that they prove more than a catalogue. Beneath them all is the awareness of "rootedness" which any place could provoke:

> But here
> In the fog-sodden fields, under the rain-eaten
> Dish-clout of the dykes, among the wrack and rubble
> Of the gull-rummaged estuary, or hidden behind
> The one-eyed wink of the ticket-seller's window—here
> Is the root of a race, clamped tight to the rock,
> Wringing from the earth its few last drops of green
> Long years after the once-tall trunk is down.

The realization that much of his subject matter was at hand in his own town perhaps struck Nicholson when he was able not only to accept the fact of his own physical limitations due to ill health but also to arrive beyond acceptance at a feeling that, in essentials, he was not at all limited. What was needed was a willingness to accept things as they were and make the most of them. The poem "The Pot Geranium," begun in 1949, is the poetic rendering of Nicholson's imaginative transcendence of his limitations and of his coming to terms with the town in which he was to continue to live.

The freshness and vigor of the poem's opening are noteworthy. The scene is set in brisk lines which proclaim an emancipation from the dictates of a preconceived meter (Nicholson's aim was, in fact, to produce "good speech" rather than "verse") and which confidently accommodate both metaphorical expression and a colloquial straightforwardness:

> Green slated gables clasp the stem of the hill
> In the lemony autumn sun; an acid wind
> Dissolves the leaf-stalks of back-garden trees,
> And chimneys with their fires unlit
> Seem yet to puff a yellow smoke of poplars.
> Freestone is brown as bark, and the model bakery
> That once was a Primitive Methodist Chapel
> Lifts its cornice against the sky.

Looking from his window, Nicholson sees a box kite riding high in the air. This descriptive detail has the symbolic force of human aspiration, but it also represents a freedom of physical activity from which the poet, confined to his bedroom, is barred. The ensuing lines seem to telescope the present and the period in the early 1930s when Nicholson spent fifteen months in bed in his sanatorium in the New Forest:

> The ceiling
> Slopes over like a tent, and white walls
> Wrap themselves around me, leaving only
> A flap for the light to blow through. Thighs and spine
> Are clamped to the mattress and looping springs
> Twine round my chest and hold me. I feel the air
> Move on my face like spiders, see the light
> Slide across the plaster; but wind and sun
> Are mine no longer, nor have I kite to claim them,
> Or string to fish the clouds.

But what the poet does have is his pot geranium, and the sight of it makes him realize that his limitations are only surface ones. Just as the apparently staid window-box plant "Contains the pattern, the prod and pulse of life/ Complete as the Nile or the Niger," so he, despite the restraints imposed by illness, is also the sum of all life and therefore does not need "to stretch for the straining kite." By extension, the image of the pot geranium stands also for Millom, itself a microcosm of the larger world. The poem's conclusion is hyperbolic, yet the

[83]

hyperbole represents a real truth: travel is not necessary when the imagination can grasp the universal implications of the ordinary:

> My ways are circumscribed, confined as a limpet
> To one small radius of rock; yet
> I eat the equator, breathe the sky, and carry
> The great white sun in the dirt of my finger-nails.

"The Pot Geranium" is, though in no pejorative sense, a self-conscious poem. Nicholson is justifying both himself and the value of his local experience. Having done so, he can in "Millom Old Quarry" look more specifically at Millom itself and reproduce something of its townsfolk's way of talking. The first stanza is a deliberate attempt to let local speech find utterance in a poem. Though it is not mainly Nicholson who speaks, his composing such a stanza indicates in itself his wish to declare himself a Millom man instead of, more generally, a Cumberland poet:

> "They dug ten streets from that there hole," he said,
> "Hard on five hundred houses." He nodded
> Down the set of the quarry and spat in the water
> Making a moorhen cock her head
> As if a fish had leaped. "Half the new town
> "Came out of yonder—King Street, Queen Street, all
> "The houses round the green as far as the slagbank,
> "And Market Street, too, from the Crown allotments
> "Up to the Station Yard."—"But Market Street's
> "Brown freestone," I said. "Nobbut the facings;
> "We called them the Khaki Houses in the Boer War,
> "But they're Cumberland slate at the back."

This matter-of-fact description prompts the poet to reflect about the connection between the rock from which the houses came and the human life which they contained—"So much that woman's blood gave sense and shape to/ Hacked from this dynamited combe." What begins as a physical description of Millom develops, therefore, into a universal picture of human growth and decay:

I saw the town's black generations
Packed in their caves of rock, as mussel or limpet
Washed by the tidal sky; then swept, shovelled
Back in the quarry again, a landslip of lintels
Blocking the gape of the tarn.

Despite the visual origin of so much of Nicholson's poetry and despite his very real interest in surface detail, what Nicholson basically concerns himself with in this regional group of poems in *The Pot Geranium* is what lies beneath the surface, for what is there gives the surface its human relevance. The urge to penetrate the surface of a place, not to reach the rock beneath, but to reach something which, from the viewpoint of the short individual life, is even deeper, is nowhere more apparent than in the poem "Old Main Street, Holborn Hill, Millom," first published in 1952. It begins with a picture of the street at night seen as a stage set, all its local individuality rubbed out by the darkness: "A property staircase leans/ Against a door that's a palace or a pub/ As the plot demands, and hessian walls hang slack/ In the dim wash of the street-lamps." Predictable after this "scene-painting" would be an assertion that by day the street appears in its true colors—a conclusion resembling that of "From Walney Island." Instead, Nicholson says that neither by night nor by day is a place seen as it actually is:

This shadow-play, this make-believe,
Has no intention to deceive:
When memory or morning restores the daytime order
To the Plough Inn, the garage, the Institute,
The Spiritualist Room, the licensed grocer's—then
What the full sun reveals is no
More real, more solid than this.

The visual appearance of a place is not the point. Both night and day offer only approximations of "the truth beneath it all," which is as apprehensible to a blind man as it is to a man with sight. For the truth, like the blind man's understanding which comes by touching, is a feeling: truth is inside, not outside. Before a place means anything, human love must exist to understand it; and the last lines of the poem act out, in their diminishing lengths, the process by which appearances are penetrated until the "something underneath" is revealed:

> Shape and appearance burst and branch and fade;
> Clock-time and season fluctuate and fall
> Like an organic river pouring from above,
> And fingers touch the truth beneath it all;
> Beneath the shape, the wall, beneath the wall, the stone,
> Beneath the stone, the idea of a stone,
> Beneath the idea, the love.

The fundamental reality—something subjective rather than objective—which is given the name of "love" is defined less emotionally in "On Being a Provincial" as the idea of home. In the sense that every place is "home" to somebody, all places are alike: "Imagine two people at two different points on the surface of a huge globe, a globe as big as the moon, and think of all the enormous area over which they can wander and yet never find one another. Yet if each of them were to drive a shaft perpendicularly beneath his feet, then, no matter where the two started, they would meet at a common centre. That common centre, in the earthly life of all people and all nations, is home."

Nicholson's love for his home town is very clear from his poetry. Except briefly, to record talks for the British Broadcasting Corporation studios in Manchester, or to give poetry readings, usually in other parts of the North of England, he rarely leaves it. In 1952, he described Millom as "a place that seems to belong to me like an outer layer of clothing, so that anywhere else I feel not properly dressed."[39] For Nicholson to see Millom as a microcosm of the world is not, perhaps, a great challenge to his imagination. Indeed, some might even suspect that his universal conclusions are a convenient cover for his indulgence of a narrow, local patriotism. When, therefore, Nicholson writes about another place (and for him to do so is exceptional, unless that place be in the Lake District), the reader looks at the result with particular care to see whether Nicholson's notion about the underlying likeness of all places can apply to an initially alien place. A reassuring indication of Nicholson's consistency and sincerity is the poem "Near Widnes" (a town in South Lancashire). Nicholson's first reaction, however, is an honest "provincial" puzzlement, expressed in the very revealing simile "All this is foreign as London." To a Cumbrian, the landscape has a disorientating lack of contour; and his prejudice against it is amusingly shown in the last phrase of his description:

> A row
> Of lombardy poplars, and beyond and over
> A landscape flat as a council survey: no
>
> Elevation, square fields painted on paper,
> Ruled roads and hedges; here and there
> A pithead or a crane or a bare tree
>
> Pencilled like a symbol. The poplars switch their branches,
> Flicking the cobwebs from the clouds, embarrassed still, unreconciled
> To feeling Lancashire about their roots.

But, just as the rock and the "love" unite all places, so does the "familiar wind" which blows the same way everywhere: "—wind that,/ Mingling marsh and mountain in the same mist,/ Pours out one single syphoning of brine/ From Windermere to Wigan." The alliteration assists in shifting the emphasis to what places have in common; and what they do have in common is defined, lightly, in religious terms. The "cosmopolitan air" admits no boundaries and "All language sounds alike/ To birds and God—all dialect, local names,/ Pet-nouns and proverbs." While Nicholson's own initial sense of strangeness in the Lancashire landscape tacitly allows his readers a like reaction to Millom, his final acceptance of what he sees "near Widnes" suggests that they in their turn should be able to see Millom *sub specie aeternitatis.*

The reference to God in "Near Widnes," like Nicholson's description in "On Being a Provincial" of London as "one of heaven's provincial towns," is a reminder that Nicholson is a poet whose religious beliefs provide the foundation for his attitude to the world around him. His regional poems in *The Pot Geranium* are fairly obviously the poems of a religious man. Because by this time he had no doubt found himself able to engage his whole personality in his local subject matter (an engagement made easier because he had developed a poetic language closer to everyday speech), very few poems in *The Pot Geranium* express religious attitudes in isolation.

Two religious poems, "A Garden Enclosed" and "A Turn for the

[87]

Better," are worthy of note. They spring from Nicholson's primary impulse to describe what is seen and then move on from it to a religious conclusion. They also place their Christian subjects firmly in a Millom context. In 1951, Nicholson wrote to George Every that "For some time now I've been thinking of a series of short descriptive lyrics of Millom life, possibly seen through the eyes of a boy, and now it occurs to me that I might construct a series of scenes of the boyhood of Christ."[40] In this idea can be clearly seen Nicholson's wish to link his local environment and his religious interests; but, of the projected series, only these two poems were written. "A Garden Enclosed" was prompted by an incident in the Apocalyptic Gospels where Christ fashioned clay birds and breathed life into them, but the local description has little energy (except the rather factitious energy of stanza two), and the references to the "bright knees" of the Holy Child who "eena-meena-mumbles" words have an embarrassing pseudo-naiveté.

Far more successful as a poem is "A Turn for the Better," which records "the incident of the world standing still at the Nativity."[41] The poem formed part of the Contemporary Arts Exhibition of Twentieth Century Poetry at the 1951 Festival of Britain, and Nicholson thinks it the best of his shorter religious poems. It stems from the phrase "Now I Joseph was walking and I walked not" in the Apocryphal Book of James, but the Joseph of the poem is Nicholson himself, who is walking among the Millom allotments; and this localization, with all its confidence in the meaningfulness of the most ordinary details to the loving eye, gives strength and conviction to the metaphysical vision of the last part of the poem. The poem's mysticism, its glimpse of the eternal, is firmly rooted in the particularities of the physical world:

> The clouds were mauve as a crocus, peeling back petals,
> And a sparse pollen of snow came parping down
> On the bare ground and green-house groins and dun
> Tight-head chrysanthemums crumpled by the frost.
> The cock in the hen-run blustered to its perch
> On the lid of the swill bucket, rattled its red
> At the fluttering flakes, levered its throat open—
> And not a croak creaked out.

All movement—of snow, of drifting dead leaf, of "workmen on the electric cable track"—is arrested to emphasize the momentousness of

[88]

Christmas morning. By a rapid telescoping of time—expressed characteristically in terms of geological process, but a reversed one—Nicholson returns to the world before the Year One, to "that minute" when the temporal was intersected by the eternal:

> The tree grew down
> Into its sapling self, the sapling into the seed.
> Cobbles of wall and slate of rafters
> Were cleft and stratified again as rock,
> And the rock un-weathered itself a cloud-height higher,
> And the sea flowed over it. A brand-new now
> Stretched on either hand to then and someday,
> Might have and perhaps.

In the last lines, the expectant fixity is broken; the image of "shillings" returns the reader to the present; but the present is now transfigured in the light of the meaning given it by Christ's birth. The "shillings" are not just a simile for the snow but an everyday symbol of the immense value of the Incarnation. The temporal, once pierced by the eternal, is itself given an eternal dimension; and the simple, short phrase reserved for the end of the poem strikes with a poignancy and force gained from its contrast with the longer abstract line which immediately precedes it and with the imaginative glimpse of centuries of human and natural life which are its context:

> Then suddenly the cock
> Coughed up its crow, the robin skittered off,
> And the snow fell like a million pound of shillings.
> And out in the beginning always of the world
> I heard the cry of a child.

The Pot Geranium contains a new category of poems in Nicholson's work. This category, consisting of six poems grouped together, may most conveniently be labeled "astronomical," though astronomy is less their subject than the impulse behind them. In this category, "The Motion of the Earth," which is most closely linked with the regional poems of the volume, starts from the idea that the brightness of daylight inevitably changes to darkness as the earth moves; but this idea is used not as a symbol of the decay inherent in change, but of the way in which, unseen by man, the context in which he lives is constantly

[89]

altering. The implication is that, if man could realize this change imaginatively, his life would be refreshed. The positive conclusion of the regional poems is that all places, in human terms, are the same; the positive conclusion of this poem is that, in astronomical terms, no single place remains the same for two minutes together. Such an ending is not dissimilar in effect from that of "The Pot Geranium"—life in one place is not really limited:

> All things are new
> Over the sun, but we,
> Our eyes on our shoes, go staring
> At the asphalt, the gravel, the grass at the roadside, the door-
> step, the doodles of snails, the crochet of mortar and lime,
> Seeking the seeming familiar, though every stride
> Takes us a thousand miles from where we were before.

It may reasonably be objected, however, that such a "truth" is so remote from any grasp other than that of the intellect that the poem is little more than an extended conceit. Astronomy itself is a more remote subject even than rock. Although anyone may be carried away by the immensity of the universe, to reduce that immensity to a scale which appears relevant to life as it confronts people every day is a very difficult task.

Some of the "astronomical" poems are simply religious allegories—metaphors with a moral. Nicholson's favorite, however, "The Undiscovered Planet," expresses itself more subtly. In it appears a real attempt, if a brief one, to convey imaginatively the look of the planet:

> . . .landscape of lead
> Whose purple voes and valleys are
> Lit faintly by a sun
> No nearer than a measurable star.

The way in which the theme of the poem recalls the actual discovery of the planet Pluto helps to remove the suspicion that astronomy is merely being used as a text, and the conclusion is general enough to apply to whatever aspect of life the reader wishes:

> . . .only
> The errantry of Saturn, the wry
> Retarding of Uranus, speak
> Of the pull beyond the pattern:
> The unknown is shown
> Only by a bend in the known.

Presumably, Nicholson has in mind a religious meaning for these lines: the apprehension of God through a mystical transformation, a "bending," of everyday reality. But the conclusion suggests aptly the way in which many of Nicholson's more characteristic poems work: by taking the "known" and giving it a slight twist (as in "A Turn for the Better" and in "The Pot Geranium") a new dimension appears.

"A bend in the known" can be achieved by taking a phrase and exploring it until it yields a deeper meaning. Talking in 1964 about his methods of composition, Nicholson mentioned that "the most profitable stimulus for poems, since I have not been writing them very frequently, has been the 'remark'."[42] Nicholson has written a number of poems based on remarks in the last fifteen years; and two of the earliest examples, in *The Pot Geranium,* are worth considering because they reveal some of the strengths and weaknesses of this approach. "Five Minutes" starts from the local phrase "I'm having five minutes" (that is, a nap) and gives it a twist by ending on the death, soon after, of the man who uses it. The result is a simple irony of situation, with no particular significance. The poem is no more than an anecdote, whose point—a play on words—lies entirely in the first line and the last three. Intervening nature description provides a context, and is pleasingly colorful and whimsical; but it contributes nothing essential since the visual details neither modify nor sharpen the poem's basic juxtaposition of incidents. In a word, the imagery of the poem is decorative, not functional; and the poem may, by severe standards, be called a failure.

"Rising Five" has a similar pattern; but, because the imagery is integrated with the theme, the poem is successful. In its smooth blending of form and content it is Nicholson's favorite among his poems, and it has also proved the most popular of the poems which he chooses to read publicly. What begins as a simple childish statement

about "going on five" (the title is the common Northern dialect form
of this expression) is investigated with such thoroughness that it ends
by becoming a symbol of man's dangerous tendency to miss the present
by thinking too much on the future:

> "I'm rising five", he said,
> "Not four," and little coils of hair
> Un-clicked themselves upon his head.
> His spectacles, brimful of eyes to stare
> At me and the meadow, reflected cones of light
> Above his toffee-buckled cheeks. He'd been alive
> Fifty-six months or perhaps a week more:
> >   not four,
> But rising five.

The imagery is not only functional because the "toffee-buckled cheeks"
will be recalled by the mention of "toffee-wrappers" farther on but
because the phrase "brimful of eyes" suggests man's appetite for
experience; and the "un-clicking" of the boy's tightly curled hair links
him with the spring activity of nature described in the next stanza. Just
as the child is growing, so the seasons recur and move on, and the
description is not just a natural context but a symbolic parallel. The
alliteration and internal rhyming underline the purposeful energy of
nature and reinforce the sense of a continuous process:

> Around him in the field the cells of spring
> Bubbled and doubled; buds unbuttoned; shoot
> And stem shook out the creases from their frills,
> And every tree was swilled with green.
> It was the season after blossoming,
> Before the forming of the fruit:
> >   not May,
> But rising June.

Having established his method of parallelism and substitution,
Nicholson speeds the poem's repetitions of its basic pattern. Like a
stone thrown in a pool, the initial phrase sends widening rings of
significance:

```
       And in the sky
       The dust dissected the tangential light:
                                  not day,

       But rising night;
                        not now,
       But rising soon.
```

From these lines, the poem is seemingly intent on presenting life as a process of decay that is gradual but incapable of being halted. But the last section, though it shows the climax of that process in death, clearly implies that, though man cannot escape his part in the cycle of nature, he need not assist it by substituting anticipation for living. Death will find him soon enough without his looking for it; and he can, if he makes an effort akin to that of dropping phrases like "rising five" and saying "four" instead, appreciate the all-too-brief present moment before it vanishes:

```
       The new buds push the old leaves from the bough.
       We drop our youth behind us like a boy
       Throwing away his toffee-wrappers. We never see the flower,
       But only the fruit in the flower; never the fruit,
       But only the rot in the fruit. We look for the marriage bed
       In the baby's cradle, we look for the grave in the bed:
                                                not living,
       But rising dead.
```

The selection from *The Pot Geranium* of poems for detailed comment has tended to emphasize those which use local material with a more or less conscious intention to draw out of it a universal meaning. The years during which many of the poems of this third volume were written were for Nicholson a time when he needed to reassure himself that the subject matter immediately available in a small town could be made significant for a larger public. His success in demonstrating this significance is due in great measure to his mature poetic technique. This technique is characterized, among other things, by an ability to use rhymed verse forms only when they are appropriate, controlled spareness in the employment of alliteration, vigorous handling of speech rhythms, and greater economy of imagery. As a result, the reader is struck as much by metaphorical or symbolic aptness as by freshness of visual observation. *The Pot Geranium* is, therefore, a technical climax in Nicholson's work.

Many of the poems in the volume, however, though their technical accomplishment is no less, do not make an overt claim to universality but are simply content to deal with the material which Nicholson finds about him. Such poems include "Winter by the Ironworks", "On Duddon Marsh," and the delightful poem "Rain":

> But rain
> When it falls on sea
> Is scarcely seen or heard or smelt
> But only felt—
> As if a skelter of birds with pittering feet
> Were letting on the glass roof of the waves.
> The unsalt water falling through the passive air
> Has no identity there
> Where each drop tastes of the full Atlantic brine.
> Back again on the sea
> Rain
> Is only sea again.

Most of Nicholson's most recent poems (which are dealt with in the next chapter), spring from provincial or personal experience and often return to his childhood and youth for their inspiration, but they have a similar lack of self-consciousness. It therefore seems that, thematically, *The Pot Geranium* represents a watershed in Nicholson's work; for it is as if, having originally been content with his region (in *Five Rivers* and, in part, in *Rock Face)*, Nicholson needed to demonstrate explicitly and perhaps self-defensively his awareness of the outside world of which his region was a part. Certainly the very existence of the poem "The Pot Geranium" suggests that the later 1940s had been to some extent a period of poetic self-examination, and it may well be that Nicholson's current confidence in dealing with material drawn now not just from his own area but also from his own past life would not have been gained without an earlier, deliberate evaluation of the wider relevance of such material.

CHAPTER 4

Recent Poetry (1954-1969)

I *The Later 1950s*

A FTER *The Pot Geranium* of 1954, Norman Nicholson published no new volume of poems.[1] The reason lay simply in the drastic reduction of his poetic output: the fifteen years from 1954 to 1969 were marked by the appearance in magazines of no more than twenty-five poems by him. Between 1959 and the middle of 1965 Nicholson was completely silent as a poet, and his twenty-five uncollected poems are divided almost equally between the later years of the 1950s and the five years from 1965 through 1969. But, where the first of these two periods involved a gradual drying-up of the poetic impulse, interrupted only occasionally by a poem as good as many of those which had gone before, the poems Nicholson has written more recently indicate a significant and very lively extension of his range and his artistry because very few of these new poems fall short of the high standard established by the best of his earlier work.

Writing in about 1956 in a Northern students' magazine, Nicholson referred to himself in passing as a poet who, having reached the age of forty, had "lost his first wind" and was "not yet. . . sure of his second." Four poems which he wrote in the mid-1950s never got beyond the manuscript stage, and this fact suggests that Nicholson really did not know what he wanted to write about. Some published poems, like "Ferry on the Mersey" (1954) had no strong imaginative pressure behind them, or were simply abortive, like the strained and portentous "The Affirming Blasphemy" (1954) which, thirteen years later, Nicholson himself said he no longer understood.[2]

It seems worthwhile, therefore, to discuss only a very few poems from the late 1950s: those which represent the continued vitality, however intermittent, both of Nicholson's language and of his local subject matter. The theme of decay and rebirth as seen in nature, which

Nicholson had expressed with particular memorableness in the last section of "The Seven Rocks," continued to interest him until about 1956 and is presented with great virtuosity in the poem "Scree," which was first published in 1958 but had been written a couple of years earlier. The poem is concerned with the stratification and erosion of rock, and part of Nicholson's virtuosity consists in his rendering of rock processes by means of the extended metaphor of "a great tree." The geological stages are made easier for the layman to grasp by being described in imagery to which his imagination has more likely access, and this imagery has the advantage for the poet of providing a legitimate, natural way of compressing into a shorter time span a process which in reality lasted "a million centuries." The poem's virtuosity is even more obviously a matter of technique, for, in Nicholson's view, "much of the content. . .is conveyed physically by rhythm and sound."[3] The poem does very skillfully alternate longer and shorter rhymed lines, and within these lines is crammed the maximum number of alliterations, assonances, and internal rhymes. The following extract, describing the rock's emergence from prehistoric seas into air which begins immediately to erode it into scree of the type which rises steeply from the southern margin of Wastwater in the Lake District, vividly illustrates the ingenuity by which Nicholson tries to communicate to the reader his own excitement about geological processes:

                         Coal
              Sprang from its bole
      Like a parasitic plant; surf and sand
              Salted and
      Silted it. Yet still the blunt trunk thrust
              Out through the crust
      Shedding the paleozoic years like bark,
              While habitual, dark
      Roots hankered back to unfossiliferous blocks
              Of rocks that made the rocks.
      The wind rips off the wrap of sand till the tree stands bare
              In the hacksawing air,
      Or under the rub of water, seep and sump,
              Worn to a stump,
      Flakes away rind in a mildew of mist.

[96]

The detached, scientific attitude revealed in "Scree," which treats change as a continuous process needing only to be recognized and described, has less emotional immediacy than the lyricism of a very beautiful poem entitled "September on the Mosses," written in 1954. In it attention is focussed not on "deciduous rock" (a rather abstract concept) but on the "deciduous tide" whose status as a symbol for change would be immediately apparent to any reader. Nicholson relates changing nature to himself by at first expressing the familiar human wish to arrest it and preserve the beauty of the immediate moment:

> Wait, tide, wait;
> Let the mosses slide
> In runnels and counter-flow of rock-pool green,
> Where web-foot mud-weeds preen
> Leaves spread in the sunshine; where
> On slow air-ripples the marsh aster lays
> Innocuous snare of sea-anemone rays.

Nicholson speaks to nature almost as if it were a part of himself; and by appearing personally vulnerable to the process of change, which is something he reacts to rather than merely describes, he creates a feeling of sympathy in the reader.

The poem's second and third stanzas renew the appeal to nature to "wait," but, despite the "summerfull of light" which shines on the mosses, the tide itself is "autumnal." Using images both concise and evocative, Nicholson's description of the estuary contains within itself hints of change:

> Behind your wide-
> as-winter ebb the poplars of the waves
> Turn up their underleaves of grey.
> Thunder-blue shadows boom across the bay.

In addition to the ambiguity inherent in the natural imagery, the altering line-lengths suggest an ebb-and-flow movement, a sense of uncertainty, which work against the poet's appeal. Therefore, when the final stanza reaches the only possible conclusion, one laid down by nature herself, that change cannot be halted, Nicholson's realization of the need for change comes as less of a surprise. The reader is prepared to accept the last line's inversion of his twice-repeated request ("Wait,

[97]

tide, wait") as a viewpoint to which his mental processes have gradually been moving, rather than to dismiss it as a clever piece of pattern making:

> Deciduous tide,
> On the willow whips of inshore billows the inside
> Edge is brown. Crying "Never!"
> Delays no due tomorrow,
> And now is ever
> By being not by lasting. So
> With pride let this long-as-life hour go,
> And flow, tide, flow.

Two poems later in the decade show Nicholson as a provincial writer responding to local, rather than universal, experience; but the topicality of "Windscale" is, in effect, a general warning about the dangers of atomic power. The poem was published in November 1957, soon after the rumor of a radioactive leak at the Calder Hall (Windscale) atomic factory, only twenty miles north of Millom, had forced the inhabitants of West Cumberland to pour away milk and to burn meat supplies for fear of contamination.[4] Nicholson saw the "toadstool towers" of Calder Hall as "Stinkhorns that propagate and spore/ Wherever the wind blows." For him, the sinister unpleasantness of radioactivity was that its dangers could not be seen; it could strike, as it were, out of a clear sky. The second stanza of "Windscale" makes the most of this contrast between peaceful appearance and a poisonous reality in a series of quietly scathing antitheses, and it stresses ironically the dislocation of normal patterns of life brought about by man's search for power—a search which, it is implied, can become a perversion of Divine purpose:

> This is a land where dirt is clean,
> And poison pasture, quick and green,
>   And storm sky, bright and bare;
> Where sewers flow with milk, and meat
> Is carved up for the fire to eat,
>   And children suffocate in God's fresh air.

In "Bond Street," published in December, 1958, Nicholson returned to the interest in his home town which characterizes much of the poetry of *The Pot Geranium*. In this poem, however, he is concerned not with Millom as a microcosm of the world, nor with his own relationship to it as a writer, but simply with an aspect of its past which he deals with for its own sake. The re-creation of the past is given a dramatic framework by being presented as the answer, inside Nicholson's head, to a request for directions made by a rather cocksure, visiting insurance salesman:

> "Bond Street," I said, "Now where the devil's that?"—
> The name like one whose face has been forgotten.—
> He watched me from a proud-as-Preston hat,
> His briefcase fat with business. "See, it's written
> First on my list. Don't you know your own town?"—

Another difference from the Millom poems of *The Pot Geranium* consists in the semicomic guise in which Nicholson appears in relation to this "off-comer": in describing Bond Street to the reader, he is the poet lovingly dwelling on a local anomaly; but he assumes towards the insurance salesman the slightly malicious offhandedness of the local resident. When the salesman declines to accept his word that "'you'll sell no insurance there,' " the "I" of the poem abandons him to his fate with lines that have the effect of an ironic inward chuckle: " 'Whatever you choose,' I said. 'A mile past the square./ Then ask again. Hope you enjoy your walk.' "

The hidden joke in this reply has already been explained to the reader in the poem's central section: "Bond Street" exists only on a map. No houses were ever erected there since the street was in that part of Millom which, though intended originally as the town's center, was forgotten about when the railway company built a bridge a hundred yards farther up the line than had been expected. This development left Bond Street only

> . . .—a mouse
> And whippet thoroughfare, engineered in mud,
> Flagged with the green-slab leaves of dock and plantain,
> A free run for the milk cart to turn round
> From either of the two back-alleys shunted
> End on against it.

From his description Nicholson moves on to seeing Bond Street, briefly, in symbolic terms: though not "the first of streets" in the sense originally intended, in another sense, it is, by remaining virgin for ninety years, "the first of streets," not only preserving untarnished the "model town" aspirations of Millom's Victorian planners, but also representing the hopeful beginnings of any human endeavor:

> . . .the throstles sense
> That here is the one street in all the town
> That no one ever died in, that never failed
> Its name or promise. The iron dust blows brown.

The last phrase switches abruptly into the present, and the reader feels in the poem more than the semicomic dialogue of poet and insurance salesman. Set into this is the more serious confrontation in the poet's mind between his own town's present and its past.

II   *The 1960s*

Not long after "Bond Street" was published, nothing by Nicholson appeared for almost seven years. In retrospect, however, the nostalgia for the local past evinced by "Bond Street" may now be seen as a healthy indication of what was to occupy and invigorate the poems which followed his long silence. These poems, about a dozen up to 1969, extend his range both in technique and in subject matter; but his new emphasis on family and local history, and on the memories of childhood and youth, is not wholly unexpected from a writer who has always been concerned with what lies closest to his own experience.[5] Biographically, what seems most strongly to have turned Nicholson's attention to the past were the deaths of his father in 1954 and of his last remaining uncle, aged eighty four, five years later. These events left him reflecting that "I am now the last one of the Nicholson family left in the town."[6] He was already delving into the past of Millom and his own family in his prose work, *Provincial Pleasures,* published in 1959; and in 1961 he recalled his uncles and his paternal grandmother in a Christmas article which he contributed to the *Church Times.*[7] It may be assumed that this material gradually took hold at a deeper imaginative level, for it finally emerged in the 1960s in poems of great vitality that are unified by a sense of direction which had been lacking in the work of a decade before.

The first of these new poems was "The Seventeenth of the Name," written in the early summer of 1965. A series of recollections of Nicholson's forebears and relatives, the poem comes to a point in his presentation of himself as the last of his family line. What is immediately striking about the poem is its form, which consists in the alternation of two long, flexible, unrhymed lines, which allow full scope for story telling, and two short, rhymed lines which prevent the anecdotes from rambling on, which superimpose on the speech rhythms a pattern that is visible on the page, and which give, when the poem is read aloud (and the poem needs to be spoken to be fully appreciated), the effect of a recurrent echo, now weaker, now stronger. This method of writing proves of particular value in the last part of the poem, for it permits Nicholson to use the rhymed lines to emphasize his most important points. Technically, the method has some affinity with that of Marianne Moore, a poet of whom Nicholson has always thought highly; but it is to Robert Lowell, whose family memories provided the material for *Life Studies,* that Nicholson himself feels the poem owes a broad thematic debt.

The first two-thirds of the poem, vigorously anecdotal, start with Nicholson's grandmother, then present fourteen uncles in sections of varying length:

>My uncle Jack
>Played full-back
For the Northern Union and went in second wicket for the First
>Eleven.
One August Monday he smacked a six clean into an excursion train—
>"Hit in from here
>To Windermere,"
My grandmother said. He broke his spine down the mine and died
>below ground
(His family's prided loss on the iron front),[8]
>Left, "Not to Mourn,"
>A daughter, born
After he died, and a widow who held to his name for fifty years.

The anecdotes build up the sense of a long family tradition which paralleled the century-long industrial development of Millom, but they are given their particular, personal significance by Nicholson's realization, provoked most of all by the "what-are-you-going-to-do-about-it/ Memorandum" of his father's gravestone,

[101]

that (as he expressed it in a letter) "...the family has died out and...I've done nothing to perpetuate it or, indeed, to help the growth of the town in the way that my grandparents did."[9] This realization is expressed in the mixed gravity and exasperation of the final lines, which add to the poem's list of anecdotes an overtone of lamentation and tribute. Though the poem itself is Nicholson's own contribution, by celebrating it, to his family tradition, he seems to see the poem, with a certain sympathetic impatience, as a negative substitute for what his forebears might more easily have understood—a child who would carry on the tradition into later generations:

> Step on the gravel and the stones squeak out
> "Nicholson, Nicholson."
> Whereupon
> Grandmother, grandfather, father, seven known
> And six clocked-out-before-me uncles stare
> From their chimneyed heaven
> On the seventeenth
> Of the name, wondering through the holy smother where the family's
> got to.
> And I, in their great-grand-childless streets, rake up for my reply
> Damn all but hem
> And haw about them.

The personal poignancy and the degree of self-criticism in this passage call to mind Yeats's famous lines prefacing *Responsibilities* (1914):

> Pardon that for a barren passion's sake,
> Although I have come close on forty-nine,
> I have no child, I have nothing but a book,
> Nothing but that to prove your blood and mine.

But the comparison with Yeats should not be pressed too far. Although there are dangerous implications about the last two lines of Nicholson's poem which would, if pursued, dangerously weaken the poem's *raison d'etre* by undervaluing the recollections of which it mostly consists, the colloquialism of the phrase employed is more lighthearted, suggesting that Nicholson may be echoing the possible thoughts of his dead relatives as much as expressing a view of his own. The irritation of the

[102]

"I" is natural but temporary; and, when one considers that the writing of "The Seventeenth of the Name" liberated Nicholson's dormant poetic energy and suggested a thematic potentiality in his family and local past which he subsequently exploited, it need not be taken to imply a deprecation in advance of the rest of his more recent work.

Nicholson commemorates two of his forebears in detail in two poems, "The Cock's Nest" and "Have You Been to London?" "The Cock's Nest"—written in March, 1968, in memory of his father's death fourteen years before in February—is a restrained but very moving poem that avoids the risk of sentimentality by the use of natural imagery. The poem describes how, early in 1954, a cock wren built a nest for its mate in the backyard of Nicholson's home:

> It found a niche
> Tucked behind the pipe of the bathroom outflow,
> Caged in a wickerwork of creeper; then
> Began to build:
> Three times a minute, hour after hour,
> Backward and forward to the backyard wall,
> Nipping off neb-fuls of the soot-spored moss
> Rooted between the bricks.

These homely details are functional: the minute observation suggests the importance to the bird of its own purposeful activity and also the significance of it in terms of human family life. The poem turns on the theory that the cock bird builds a number of nests, in any one of which the hen may choose to lay her eggs; and the poem's point is that "she didn't choose our yard." The final lines quietly bring home the metaphorical relevance of the resulting empty nest to the sense of loss felt by Nicholson at his father's death, and the reader sees how the earlier description of the cock's nest building has been deliberately dwelt upon in order to throw into relief, with painful irony, the emptiness of the poem's terse conclusion:

> And as March gambolled out, the fat King Alfred sun[10]
> Blared down too early from its tinny trumpet
> On new-dug potato-beds, the still bare creeper,
> The cock's nest with never an egg in,
> And my father dead.

The indirect approach adopted by "The Cock's Nest," which

depends on the emotional power of selected images, is found also in one of Nicholson's finest and most moving poems, "Have You Been to London?" which was written in the summer of 1966. On one level, the poem represents Nicholson's recollections of his paternal grandmother to whom, when he was at Millom Secondary School, he used to read every Saturday: though he did not know it at the time, she herself could not read. "Saturday's stint" of reading is vividly re-created in the second section in which the abrupt, breathless rhythms of the brash schoolboy's arrival contrast with the greater formality, heightened by the internal rhyme, of the lines describing the old-fashioned living room:

> I blew into the room, threw
> My scholarship cap on the rack;
> Wafted visitors up the flue
> With the draught of my coming in—
> Ready for Saturday's mint imperials,
> Ready to read
> The serial in *Titbits*, the evangelical
> Tale in the parish magazine,
> Under the green
> Glare of the gas,
> Under the stare of my grandmother's Queen.

The visual details—the severe portrait of Queen Victoria, the "china dogs on the mantleshelf"—combine with the deflation of the young boy's cocky assurance by means of the semiproverbial dig at his careless manners (" 'They shut doors after them/ In London,' she said") to produce a likeness of a straight-backed, sarcastic but not unkind grandmother who would be promptly recognized by many English readers. So far, the poem is no more than a dryly affectionate personal reminiscence, an amusing confrontation between youth and age. But the last ten lines, harking back pointedly to the "draught" created by the boy's entry and to the kettle which, when three generations of Nicholsons were simultaneously alive, was always "simmering on the bright black lead" of the fireplace, draw out the hidden, sadder implications of what seemed, in the poem's first section, only descriptive phrases. Nicholson's "virtuosity of print" now becomes symbolic of the destructive effects which seem, willy-nilly, to have accompanied education on the warm, close family feeling embodied in his illiterate grandmother. In regretting her absence, Nicholson seems also to regret the vanishing of a way of life whose virtues are only realized when it is too late. The poet, years after, is left as the last of his family in a world for whose changed values his literacy is no comfort, and he conveys with poignant impressionism his sense of bafflement and regret:

> . . .and the generations boiled down to one
> And the kettle burnt dry
> In a soon grandmotherless room;
> Reading for forty years
> Till the print swirled out like a down-catch of soot
> And the wind howled round
> A world left cold and draughty,
> Un-latched, un-done
> By all the little literate boys
> Who hadn't been to London.

In his more recent peoms, Nicholson still writes as a provincial in that he takes whatever comes to hand in the life around him or in his local and personal memories; but, where the "key" poems in *The Pot Geranium* are in a sense commentaries on themselves, seeking not only to express their materials but also to justify their use, "the new poems don't [relate their material to an explicit provincial attitude]. . .they take it for granted—as if. . .I had drawn up the scheme through which I see life and the world and could now just forget about it, or, rather, could feel it without having to talk about it."[11] Nevertheless, Nicholson's poem "The Black Guillemot," written in July, 1967, shows that, in himself, he is no less aware than he was fifteen years ago of being a provincial poet who possesses all that this term implies of a sense of identity with his fellow provincials.

"The Black Guillemot," which employs the method of extended allegory, leaves its human and personal application to be inferred; but the inference is not an obscure one to draw. The poem reads at first as pure description, presented in almost excessive detail, of the sea birds which Nicholson watches one evening at St. Bees Head:

> The guillemots rest
>
> Restlessly. Now and then,

> One shifts, clicks free of the cliff,
> Wings whirring like an electric-fan—
> Silhouette dark from above, with underbelly gleaming
> White as it banks at the turn—
> Dives, scoops, skims the water,
> Then, with all Cumberland to go at, homes
> At the packed slum again,
> The rock iced with droppings.

Apart from the rather jarring "electric-fan" simile, the language and the rhythm—now broken, now smooth—reproduce the bird's flight with the accuracy and literal fidelity of an observing naturalist; but the interpolation "with all Cumberland to go at" already suggests that the picture of the birds applies also to human society, whose members have the same homing instinct. The following section offers a contrasting picture of the black guillemot, the odd-man-out who is "self-subsistent as an Eskimo,/ Taking the huff if so much as a feather/ Lets on his pool and blow-hole/ In the floating pack-ice of gulls." Such a description is hardly less true of the artist, who values his independence, than it is of the "rarer auk." The point which Nicholson, however, characteristically wishes to emphasize is not the artist's difference from his fellows but his likeness to them. This concept is brought out in the final section, which takes its cue from the natural phenomenon that, in times of storm, all the birds congregate in the same place:

> But, turn the page of the weather,
> Let the moon haul up the tide and the pressure hose of spray
> Swill down the lighthouse lantern—then,
> When boats keep warm in harbour and bird-watchers in bed,
> When the tumble-home of the North Head's rusty hull
> Takes the full heave of the storm,
> The hundred white and the one black flock
> Back to the same rock.

The heavy accents and doubled rhyme of the last two lines underscore the human application which Nicholson wishes to suggest. In times of stress, which reveal the deepest human instincts, the artist and his fellow men—specifically, his fellow townsfolk—are one.

One natural form that Nicholson's sense of identity has lately taken is an interest not just in his own memories but in what might be called community memories: the past of his home town, whose prosperity sprang from the ore-bearing rock of Hodbarrow Mines. "The Riddle" deals with an incident in the 1920s when one of the small railway engines employed at Hodbarrow Mines vanished into a hole in the ground caused by mining subsidence. The title of the poem refers not to this strange incident, which is given no particular significance except in so far as its shock effect seems to have represented for Nicholson a line of demarcation between childhood and adolescence, but to the Schoolboy riddle of *"Why is a baby/ Like a railway engine?,"*[12] with which the poem begins. The poem sprang in fact from this remark, which occurred to Nicholson apropos of nothing. Its connection with the poem's eventual subject was established only after much searching of his memory: it had been said to him once by the "son of the day-shift engine driver" in whose company he had seen the engine disappear, and it had remained in his subconscious for forty-odd years to emerge in 1966 and to release in poetic form a recollection which he had already set down briefly in prose in 1959; "The land subsided. Houses collapsed; roads caved in; a railway locomotive dived out of sight into a hole which opened for it like a yawn."[13] The feeling of mute amazement experienced by the boys is sensitively conveyed in the short lines in which the poem is cast:

> We stood in the steaming
> November air
> Staring at rails
> Bent to no junction;
> And switch-point levers
> Left without function
> Swiveled eyes wide
> Down tracks of drifting shales—

After describing the way in which "the sand's slow tide" covered the scene of the accident until no sign of it was left, the poem returns to the present. The bizarre fate of "Old Rustyknob," the engine, has now become an item of Millom mythology, something which "only the old remember now,/ And only the young believe."

Just as the content of Nicholson's latest poems is less overtly provincial than that of his work of the early 1950s, so, in his own words, "their tone is lighter, much more lyrical, and flows more quickly along."[14] The "strongly forward and limpid rhythm" of "The Riddle" provides apt illustration of Nicholson's new manner of expression. In

1967 he summarized his own view of his latest poems in words that suggested the likelihood of future work on the same lines: "[They] may very well be the beginning of a period less 'important'. . .than my poems of ten years ago, but I feel that these are the poems I can now have pleasure in writing."[15]

The shape of Nicholson's poetic future, however, has become less predictable than it seemed in 1967. Until 1968, Nicholson's poems about his own history and that of his town were based, implicitly, on an assumed continuity between past and present. Millom's livelihood had been founded for the hundred years of its industrial existence on iron; and, despite the dereliction of Hodbarrow Mines, iron continued to be produced in Millom from ore imported from abroad. Nicholson's nostalgic recollections of the past (exemplified particularly in "To a Millom Musician," a bitter-sweet elegy, written in 1967, about the "down-at-heel decade" of the Depression) were therefore indulged in the context of a positive, modestly thriving communal present. In 1968, however, Millom's continuity was abruptly shattered by a government decision to close the ironworks. The effect of this decision, for a one-industry town, was crippling: instead of the "golden dole days" recalled in "To the Memory of a Millom Musician" came the leaden contemporary reality of a twenty-five percent unemployment rate, the highest in England.

It was to be expected that a poet as closely involved with his community as Nicholson would respond poetically (as well as in other ways) to the closing of the ironworks. "On the Closing of Millom Ironworks: September 1968" is a blend of elegy for a now-vanished way of life and of terse irony directed at a decision based not on industrial inefficiency but on a centralized policy of "rationalisation" which takes no account of local needs:

> Down
> On the ebb-tide sands, the five-funnelled
> Battleship of the furnaces lies bleached and rusting;
> Run aground, not foundered;
> Not a crack in her hull;
> Lacking but a loan to float her off.

The townspeople's habit of telling by the smoking chimneys of the ironworks "which way the wind is blowing" must now be unlearned, and the lack of sound in the air is deafening to those accustomed to its constant, taken-for-granted presence:

> . . .no grey smoke-tail
> Pointers the mood of the wind. The hum
> And blare that for a hundred years
> Drummed at the town's deaf ears
> Now fills the air with the roar of its silence.

Nicholson's admission that "It's beautiful to breathe the sharp night air" has a touch of conscious banality about it which suggests an ironic intention beneath its genuine, but temporary, gratitude: "sharp night air" provokes a response which in a seaside resort would be in order but which in a working town like Millom soon proves out of place. Economic stagnation is too high a price to pay for such equivocal improvement (hinted at in a rhyme whose triteness can hardly be accidental) as is produced by the absence of blowing slag dust: "The curtains will be cleaner/ And the grass plots greener/ Round the Old Folk's council flats." The pious cliché, chalked on a wall, that " 'No-one starves in the Welfare State' " is no compensation for loss of jobs, loss of pride, and the permanent disappearance of the town's very reason for existence—a disappearance which even in the Depression years was only temporary. Millom, in 1968, has reverted to its preindustrial state of a hundred years before:

> They stand
> By the churchyard gate,
> Hands in pockets, shoulders to the slag,
> The men whose fathers stood there back in '28,
> When their sons were at school with me.
> The town
> Rolls round the century's bleak orbit.

Unfortunately, the concise, controlled mixture of sorrow and anger communicated by the greater part of the poem is weakened by its conclusion which conveniently forgets the earlier statement that no smoke is visible (and thus the direction of the wind thereby unknown) in order to make rather sentimental use of dead metaphors which might better have been avoided. Nicholson's concern as a man seems on this occasion to have overcome, though pardonably, the equally vital concern of the poet for properly moving expression:

[109]

> But not a face
> Tilts upward, no-one enquires of the sky.
> The smoke prognosticates no how
> Or why of any practical tomorrow.
> For what does it matter if it rains all day?
> And what's the use of knowing
> Which way the wind is blowing
> When whichever way it blows it's a cold wind now?

The apparent finality of this situation prompts one to wonder what its effect may be on a poet who has always valued his local background and whose subject matter and imagery have always been intimately connected with it. The renewed vitality displayed by his poems of the late 1960s leaves little room for doubt that Nicholson will continue to write poetry; but it seems reasonable to suppose that "On the Closing of Millom Ironworks," in marking the end of an era for Nicholson's home town, may also have marked the end of a period in his poetic career.

CHAPTER 5

Verse Plays

THROUGHOUT Nicholson's career his publication of volumes of poetry has in effect alternated with the writing of verse plays which have appeared at almost equal intervals over a period of fifteen years. There are four plays: *The Old Man of the Mountains* (1946), *Prophesy to the Wind* (1950), *A Match for the Devil* (1955), and *Birth by Drowning* (1960). Like his poetry, Nicholson's plays derive jointly from his Christian beliefs and from his regional experience; for each play makes use either of Old Testament characters and incidents, or of an environment that is recognizably Cumberland, or both. All have been performed on a number of occasions, not only in England but in the United States. Both *Prophesy to the Wind* and *A Match for the Devil* have been staged by students at Denison University, Ohio; *The Old Man of the Mountains,* by students at Hunter College, New York. The latter play has, in addition, been translated into Welsh, Danish, and Dutch. Though Nicholson's plays are not the type to generate fashionable critical acclaim, they have enjoyed a respectable degree of practical success.

Nicholson turned to verse-drama partly because it seemed a medium by which a poet could enlarge his audience, but the one for which he has written has never been that of the metropolitan, commercial theater. What he has generally had in mind is the kind of audience found in "small towns and villages. . .ordinary lower-middle-class people in Church Halls and Methodist Sunday Schools"[1] —a less sophisticated audience and one perhaps more willing to accept what he felt best able to write: plays with an undisguised religious subject.

Nicholson had his own first theatrical experiences as a member of this type of audience, for he regularly attended the annual productions of the Millom Amateur Operatic Society. The positive element which he sensed in these unpolished performances was the rapport engendered when the "actors" were personally known to those in the body of the hall: the audience collaborated in, and partly created, the enactment on the stage. The show, in fact, was a species of ritual, like the medieval miracle and morality plays, which Nicholson described in 1960 as "the supreme example in English of drama which is played not so much *before* an audience as *for* it, on its behalf, in its stead."[2] Nicholson's own plays—with their tendency to address and involve the audience—have much in common with the "old Folk Plays," and he clearly felt that this type of play was far from being out of date: ". . . .the psychological and social need which gave rise to these ritual plays still remains, especially where people are joined together by a local patriotism or a shared purpose or belief."

On this basis of "shared belief" the revival of Christian verse-drama in the 1930s was built; and, though one presents Nicholsons's views of drama as if they were autonomous, it would be truer to say that they are one example of a general movement which favored Christian themes in drama and believed in the efficacy of verse as a dramatic medium. Nicholson's plays, though they have their own distinct and individual character, were partly prompted by, and partly fitted in with, the spirit prevalent at the time in which they began to be written. The first real stimulus to Christian verse-drama in the twentieth century had been the foundation by G.K.A. Bell, then Dean of Canterbury, of the Canterbury Festival in 1929. The most important play written for this festival was T. S. Eliot's *Murder in the Cathedral* (1935), and the power of Eliot's poetic language, together with the prestige of his literary reputation, probably did more than anything else to establish the right of religious plays to be taken seriously.

A spur to the writing of religious plays had also been given by the formation in 1929 of the Religious Drama Society and by the appointment the following year of E. Martin Browne as director of religious drama for the diocese of Chichester. Browne's name is inseparable from the revival of Christian drama: he collaborated with Eliot in the writing of *The Rock* (1934); he was closely associated with the Chichester Festival, for which Christopher Fry wrote in 1937 his first play, *The Boy with a Cart;* and in 1939 he founded the Pilgrim Players, a professional group which acted in schools, churches, village halls, prisons, and, during the period of the blitz, in air raid shelters. The audiences this group played to can hardly have been very different from those with which Nicholson was already familiar in

Millom. When, therefore, E. Martin Browne commissioned from Nicholson, in the latter years of World War II, a play which the Pilgrim Players could take on tour, Browne was giving him the ideal opportunity to write just the kind of play he was equipped to write and for the kind of audience he understood.

Three plays which Nicholson read in the 1930's influenced him in varying degrees. Dorothy Sayers's *The Zeal of Thy House*, the Canterbury Festival play for 1937, he had not greatly liked; but it may well have suggested to him the idea of a play which could present a naturalistic story while still indicating the presence of God behind the human characters. The intervention in the historical action of Dorothy Sayers's four angels has its parallel in Nicholson's Raven (the voice of God in *The Old Man of the Mountains*) and in his use of the Fells in *Birth by Drowning* to transmit God's instructions to Elisha. Andrew Young's *Nicodemus* (1937) seemed to Nicholson "direct and good," and its verse "fresh and often exhilarating."[3] Here perhaps was an example of a play which imperceptibly fused human and divine levels and which did not need to be sophisticated in order to succeed.

It was Eliot, however, who had the strongest influence; but it was the Eliot of *Murder in the Cathedral* rather than of the later plays. *Murder in the Cathedral* exemplified what was for Nicholson the most important ingredient of verse-drama, vitality of language. The use, also, of a chorus emphasized the play's ritual nature and its author's wish that the audience should participate in, rather than simply observe, the action. The play, which returned to the tradition of the Moralities, treated a religious theme unashamedly; and for Nicholson it "opened vast new territories." Eliot's later plays, with their watered-down poetic language, geared to "the ordinary, unbelieving and half-believing audience of the commercial theater,"[4] were not in line with Nicholson's deepest views; and he described *The Confidential Clerk* as "an electric radiator disguised as a coal fire."[5]

Nicholson's own plays are based implicitly on the assumption of a degree of "shared belief" in his audience, and on his local experience which he felt provided him with a natural source of poetic speech of a kind which his audience could accept without strain. Nicholson, who had read J.M. Synge, admired his dramatic language, and it was in words which are almost a paraphrase of Synge's famous Preface to *The Playboy of the Western World* (1907) that he indicated, if not his prescriptions for poetic drama generally, then at least the kind of play he himself preferred, or thought himself able, to write: ". . .up and down the world, away from cities, there are still people who speak with something of the old vitality and splendour. Behind the speech of country folk lies the imagery of the seasons; behind that of miners lies the rock; behind that of sailors lies the sea. Among such people the poet should be able to find a language, capable of the power of rhetoric and the decoration of imagery, which would yet be in touch with the essential experience of every man and woman in his audience."[6]

I   The Old Man of the Mountains

Although *The Old Man of the Mountains* was intended to be taken on provincial tour (which it later was), Nicholson's first play had its first performance in London. E. Martin Browne decided to present in 1945 a season of "New Plays by Poets" at the very small Mercury Theatre in Notting Hill Gate, where *Murder in the Cathedral* had enjoyed a year's run in 1937-38. Among the plays offered were Anne Ridler's *The Shadow Factory*, Ronald Duncan's *This Way to the Tomb*, and, later on, Christopher Fry's *A Phoenix too Frequent.* Browne's particular faith in Nicholson's play is attested by his frequent reference to it during the publicity which preceded the season and by his choice of it as the first play to be presented. Robert Speaight, who had played Becket during the initial run of Eliot's *Murder in the Cathedral,* took the part of Elijah, the "old man" of the title; and there is no doubt that Nicholson embarked as a playwright in a most encouraging atmosphere. The Mercury Theatre was exactly right for the play: a small place, intimate in atmosphere, not unlike the kind of theater which Nicholson had had in mind, yet at the same time in London and so under the eye of influential critics. Most of the play's reviews were favorable, the only serious criticism being directed at its third act, which was felt to be anticlimactic. This criticism caused Nicholson to make a number of textual changes which were incorporated in the third impression of the play in 1950. The broad outlines of the story itself remain much the same as in the acted version of the play first published in 1946; but, in fairness to Nicholson's second thoughts, this discussion refers to the 1950 text.

The Old Man of the Mountains is founded on incidents in the life of Elijah described in I Kings xvii–xviii: the prophecy of drought in Samaria, the miracle of the bin of flour and the cruse of oil, Elijah's healing of the Widow's son, his challenge to the idolater Ahab, and the final return of the rain. To the Old Testament story Nicholson has added the flesh of characterization and motive by making Elijah (who in the Bible story simply does what God tells him) into a man half-commanding, half-querulous, whose relationship to God is attended by doubts and self-reproach. Despite a comment in the *Church Times* that Nicholson had reduced Elijah from "a major to a minor prophet,"[7] the effect of the change is to make him a more sympathetic and interesting character. Similarly, Ahab is humanized from the rather wooden Bible figure (who convenes the prophets of Baal without demur) into a man partly oppressive, partly inventive, and partly defied by his tenants—one whose threatening rant seems a disguise for his disquiet at Elijah's challenge. Obadiah's function is expanded: he becomes a figure awkwardly set between the upright morality of Elijah and the practical expediency of Ahab. The widow and her son are given names, Ruth and Ben; and, to round out the play's presentation of a community, Nicholson invents the characters David, Rebecca, and Martha.

These elaborations cannot be said to tamper with the Bible story, and it is worth noting that Nicholson makes no attempt to deny the three miracles described in his source: the bringing back to life of Ben, the continual replenishing of the flour and (in Nicholson's version) the milk, and the coming of the rain. Only the last can be "explained away" as a natural event. The others are uncompromisingly miraculous, and the fundamentalist logic of their retention is quite clear. If, as Obadiah says in the Interlude, "this is the land of the one omnipotent God," then there are no limits to God's omnipotence, ancient or modern. The miracles are retained partly, no doubt, for their dramatic value but also, more importantly, because of their reality: they are an aspect of the divine will as it is revealed to men.[8] The fact that, in the play, God speaks to Elijah through the Raven prepares the audience to accept the other miracles, and this acceptance is made easier by the play's unsophisticated rural setting.

Nicholson has made his basic departure from the Old Testament story in his use of a rural setting and not of a re-created Samaria. The Cumberland dales setting, however, is not just a way of dressing up an old story. It is rather that Nicholson saw in the materialist greed of the modern world (already indicated in the poems "Egremont" and "Cleator Moor") a situation for which the struggle of Elijah and Ahab provided a convenient paradigm. One of the earliest speeches of the Raven makes quite clear the play's contemporary didactic intention:

> You have forgotten that the becks are not made nor bred;
> They are not to be expected nor taken for granted;
> That water is a gift and also rain.
> All this has happened before among the hills of Samaria—
> There was Elijah the prophet and Ahab the ruler,
> There was a greedy and a godless people.
> And what of you? Are you not like them?
> Here in a northwest corner of a northwest island
> Is not the story of Samaria enacted again?
> The God of Gold, the God of Power,
> Is not that God acknowledged again in your hearts?
> Therefore Elijah the prophet shall speak once more,
> Here in a northwest corner of a northwest island. (12)

In effect, however, the play is set in "a land which is both Samaria and Cumberland";[9] the homely speech of the dales folk establishes the latter context, Bible phrases (such as Elijah's "As the Lord God lives/ Before whom I stand"), and the retention of the original biblical names remind the audience of the former. On the whole, this dual method works fairly well. In "departing" from the Old Testament setting, Nicholson has not really moved very far; since in his view the Cumberland dales and Old Testament Palestine had in common an "essentially rural and agricultural" economy.[10]

The play's central theme is a universal Christian one: the opposition of the true God and the false gods, who are championed, respectively, by Elijah and Ahab. There is also a more "inward" theme, however: pride. The conclusion of the play is not a simple victory for Elijah; it is not only Ahab's pride, but Elijah's, which is reduced. The prophet has his own kind of pride, which leads him to make his own kind of mistakes; and, when Ahab finally sees life in a proper perspective (by granting the power of God), he too can have something to offer; and Elijah then has to "roll up his sleeves and get to work like anyone else."[11]

The presentation of Elijah as a Cumbrian statesman-farmer and Ahab as a rich, grasping landowner of the dales enables Nicholson to sharpen the opposition between them and to give it a twentieth-century application by making them stand for two different attitudes to farming, or, to put it in the play's underlying religious terms, two different attitudes to the God-given natural world. Here Nicholson was greatly influenced by the

[116]

agrarian policies of the *New English Weekly,* which spoke out strongly against such things as water pollution, dustbowl farming, too mercenary an attitude to productivity in farm animals, and the wholesale devastation of land through indiscriminate tree-felling. Ahab's greed is seen right from the start when he sends David to chop down Ruth's ash tree for timber and when he proposes a sort of farmers' cooperative to force up the price of eggs and other farm produce. He expounds his philosophy of farming in a speech whose sequence of harsh verbs condemns him as a profiteer:

> We must see that the land is made to pay. . .
> Dig chemicals in your soil, comb the fields
> Till the last ear of corn is hooked from the grain;
> Make your beasts earn their keep, squeeze the last pint
> Of milk from the cows, and work your horses
> Till they are only fit for the knacker's yard. (19)

In such a materialistic context, in which only Ruth murmurs that "money's not everything," Elijah makes his first appearance; and it is hardly surprising that he should doubt his status as a prophet. He feels cut off from God; and, without a firm faith, his life as a sheep farmer has no meaning for him:

> The Lord has turned his back.
> Ahab has the power, and Ahab derides my words.
> My farm is left desolate, my sheep
> Wander untended among the ghylls.

His words are moving, but defeatist; as an earlier speech (24—25) makes it clear, he has left his farm by his own choice. Yet God's messenger, the Raven, whose voice he echoes unawares in prophesying drought, still visits him; and in a sort of mime the Raven gives him food and tells him to sleep "while the sun/ Winds its rope round the summer, tying tighter the knot/ Till the land is strangled with heat." While he sleeps, the voice of the Beck acts out its own drying-up in lines which recall Part V of *The Waste Land:* "Only a last/ Drip, drip,/ A last/ last/ drop/ then/ stop" (27—28).

These slowing-down lines indicate the passing of months, and Elijah's sleep allows the play to modulate into colloquial prose. When he wakes and goes to Ruth's house, he speaks not even like a prophet who doubts himself but simply like an ordinary man with a habit of down-to-earth simile: "Hallo, Ruth. I wonder if I could trouble you for a glass of water. I'm feeling as dry as a haddock." The purpose of such language is not to belittle the Old Testament figure of Elijah, nor does the contrast with his earlier mode of expression betray a lack of unity in Nicholson's rendering of his character. Its point is that "a prophet is only an instrument";[12] when God is not using him, he is just like his neighbors.

The remainder of Act I presents the two aspects of Elijah. His reaction to "his" miracle of the flour and the milk is a kind of bewilderment, and the episode is treated semicomically; but the bringing to life of Ben calls up all Elijah's resources of faith. The suspense is prolonged not simply to make the most of its dramatic effect but to bring forth the inner struggle of Elijah to reestablish contact with the God whom he now feels he has betrayed. His appeal over Ben's body has the moving eloquence of absolute humility:

Let not Thy wrath fall upon this lad.
I own that I have failed Thee, that I have doubted Thy voice.
Now indeed I know that it was Thy voice. Oh,
There is nothing in the world so deaf as I have been. Yet Lord
Let Thy will be shown once more through me, once more let it be
    known,
Through me, Thy servant, that Thou art God in the dale.
Not for myself I ask. Do with me,
Lord, as Thou wilt. But let this lad live again. (32–33)

The raising of Ben, which is not dwelt on with any sentimental piety, restores Elijah's faith: it never afterwards ebbs so low as it was shown to have done at the start of the play.

Act II, nevertheless, demonstrates that no such faith is yet possible for Ahab. Indeed, though Elijah is reconciled to Ahab at the end of the play, Nicholson avoids the temptation to present Ahab as a changed man. All that really happens is that Ahab's practicality is accorded by Elijah a place in the scheme of things after God has been shown to be master of that scheme. Ahab may reasonably be considered to remain a materialist to the end, for his speech shows clearly a kind of emphasis which he cannot avoid:

No, *you* brought the rain,
I grant you that. Whether it was God or your prayers

Or the blind chance of a summer thunderstorm
I cannot tell. But the rain came—that's what matters. (79)

In Act II, with the issue between him and Elijah still unresolved, Ahab's practicality is presented with more brutal irony. Rebecca struggles for possession of a can of water which Martha has brought from a spring discovered by Elijah. The symbolism of the spilling in which the greedy struggle culminates is lost on Ahab. His remedy for the drought remains the same: "If there's water there I'll find it if I've got to blow the rock to smithereens" (44). For Elijah "there is no remedy/ But the remedy of the heart which is called repentance. And repentance means/ Humbly to accept the gift and grace of the seasons,/ To tend the earth like a mother not a slave." Obadiah's suggestion of a compromise, even a running-in-harness of these two philosophies (the suggestion is expressed in an unconscious parody of politicians' language) drives the exasperated Elijah to a confrontation with Ahab. The people are to meet on Carmel Fell to decide once and for all "Whether they'll keep God's way and obey his precepts,/ Or follow Ahab and guzzle on the bread of the land/ Like rats gnawing the sacrament" (49).

After a stylized Interlude on Carmel, in which Obadiah describes the elemental mountain landscape and, on the other side of the stage, Elijah prays to God to declare his power, Act III returns to the village where the dales folk recall their awareness of some supernatural presence on Carmel and Elijah's talk of hearing "the sound/ Of an abundance of rain." The predicted rain, however, is some time in coming; and the game of drafts with which Elijah and Ben occupy their waiting serves to bring out the contrast between Elijah's nervous fear that his premonitions of rain have played him false and the serene confidence of the boy. When the rain finally comes, growing from "a cloud no bigger than a man's hand" into thunder and lightning and a soaking downpour, Elijah's relief is evident in the exuberance of his description:

> Now Thy words go bumping round the sky
> Like huge empty barrels on the cobbles of the clouds,
> Bursting the water-butts and tipping the gullies
> On the fells and the woodland and the dale. Now
> The thirsty mouths of the trees are licking their tongues
> Into the wet soil, and grasses suck the rain
> Into their stems, and the great humps of the hills
> Gulp the water like whales and spout it out
> Through the many snouts of springs and fountains.(77)

The play does not end here, however. The rain is more than God's private signal to Elijah that his waiting was not in vain; it is real rain, part of the scheme of nature. Elijah's role as prophet should now be superseded by his occupation of farmer, but Elijah makes the mistake of patronizing the practicality of his neighbors, which is juxtaposed ironically with his own high-flown religious contemplation:

ELIJAH. The women have gone; their hearts are stitched to their
    fingers.
    Only you and I, Obadiah, who watch the hours
    Alone on the fells with the helm wind and the Lord,[13]
    Know how the shafts of eternity strike to the soul.
OBADIAH. Aye, Elijah, I'd like to have a crack. But I'll have to get
    along and fix the mill-wheel while the beck's in flood.(81)

The irony is against Elijah, not Obadiah. Elijah, who is in danger of crediting himself with the miracle of the rain, has his pretensions deflated when the Raven enters and instructs him to "Return and seek a liturgy in your labours." Elijah's last words in the play, when he suddenly recollects the needs of his farm and his sheep, are appropriately in prose; and the play ends, as it began, with the voice of the Beck, now flowing again, and the voice of the Raven, which now expresses God's approval of human beings who, however unconsciously, have become aware of Him and are properly related to the world in which they live. The Raven's words of commendation for the virtues of ordinary life and labor have an Eliot ring; but the sentiments they express are deeply characteristic of Nicholson:

        In the preoccupations of day by day
        They shall find grace and a glint of glory,
        And blossom yearly like the damsons.

In his article "The Abandoned Muse" (1948), Nicholson said that, though audiences have been conditioned by their experience of prose drama to expect "a true, or at least plausible, representation of life," the verse-dramatist is free within this realistic convention to "practice verbal and technical experiments." *The Old Man of the Mountains* achieves this blend of convention and experiment by framing, or punctuating, the naturalistic action with speeches by the Raven which make its religious meaning and its contemporary relevance quite clear and also by using a mixture of prose and verse to indicate what may be called "different levels of significance" during the course of the play.

Eliot's view, expressed in his essay *Poetry and Drama* (1951), was that "a mixture of prose and verse in the same play is generally to be avoided" except where the playwright "wishes to transport the audience violently from one plane of reality to another." Although Nicholson's transitions are, on the whole, smooth, they certainly do indicate a change of plane. Nicholson's use of a mixed form does not simply divide characters rigidly into those who speak verse and those who speak prose; for Elijah in his prophet role speaks in verse, but he is also a countryman with a countryman's downright speech. Similarly, characters like Rebecca, Ruth, and Obadiah speak colloquially of dale affairs among themselves; but, when they are caught up in the religious dialectic of the play, they slip easily into verse. Only the Raven and the Beck use verse exclusively: the Beck, because it stands for inanimate nature for which a stylized onomatopaeic expression is appropriate; the Raven, because, as spokesman of the divine will, he exists on the same plane throughout the play. The only human character who speaks solely in prose is Ben, perhaps because Nicholson felt that verse would sound self-conscious in the mouth of a boy, perhaps because he did not wish to risk sentimentality by underlining Ben's position as a "Wordsworthian" child who, because of his vision of "cloud-faces" when "dead," is closer to God than his elders.

Eliot's objection to the use of both prose and verse stemmed from his feeling that audiences needed to be lulled into accepting verse; therefore "to introduce prose dialogue would only be to distract their attention from the play itself to the medium of its expression." Nicholson, with different audiences in mind, disagreed with Eliot's tentative approach to verse;[14] but he also felt that the colorfulness of his prose made it close enough to verse to render transitions easy: " ... my country or small town colloquialisms are so near to poetry that I think they fit very well into a verse play, while my poetic flights (especially Elijah himself) are near enough to Methodist local preaching for the older-fashioned audience to feel at home with them."[15]

Nicholson's assertion about his prose can be agreed with if one accepts Synge's view of "poetry" as speech which is "as fully flavoured as a nut or an apple."[16] The prose of *The Old Man of the Mountains* does have considerable zest, and often it adds a useful leaven of comedy. A certain amount of dialect ("owt," "champion," "have a crack," "fratching") and the use of similes drawn from local experience (like Ben's "I'm as full as a black pudding" and Martha's description of Elijah as "obstinate as a tup") help to root the action in a specific place and thereby to give particular relevance to a universal theme. The critic need only look at the language of the "Wakefield Master" in, for instance, the medieval *Second Shepherds' Play* for a precedent. Sometimes, however, Nicholson's local effects can be overdone. A pseudo-proverbial expression like Martha's "If £5 notes were as common as trees I'd buy myself a fish and chip shop" (14), though sardonic in its context, makes the error of defining in a too-limited fashion the kind of audience at which the play is aimed; and David's allusion to Elijah, "If Old Moore yonder had kept his gob shut it'd have been a gay sight better for everyone" (66), is too crude a bid for a cheap laugh.

Probably the main reason for Nicholson's employment in the play of both verse and prose is to allow its twin aspects—Old Testament story and Cumberland setting—to be presented credibly side by side without either aspect blurring too much at the edges. A verse convention is appropriate for the higher level of action derived directly from the Bible story, but the dales folk would sound stilted if, for ordinary purposes, they spoke other than a credible everyday prose. Without its prose, the play would lack the local flavor which gives the religious theme its application; without the explicit moral statements of the verse passages, the prose of the dales folk would seem rambling and the presentation of their lives would lack significance.

The thematic burden of the play is carried by a verse of considerable flexibility. The speeches of the Raven resemble the text of a sermon, and his introduction of himself to the audience, "I am the Raven," has the simple directness of God in the Miracle Plays. Elijah, when sure of himself, speaks with the same biblical air of complete authority:

> Other cities there are,
> Where the flocks feed in the streets, and weasels hunt in the alleys,
> And the market places are a desolation of nettles.
> There the ivy throttles the long necks of the columns
> And the throstles drop their lime on the painted pavements,
> And like them also
> Shall be your house if you forsake the laws of the Lord.[22]

The verse also serves to describe a scene, making visible a setting which a small theater lacking scenery could not otherwise suggest. The

Raven's first speech is a fine example of Nicholson's ability not simply to "paint a picture" but to make the audience feel it; there is a skillful repetition of verbal patterns as the eye is led downwards as by the closing-in of a camera lens:

> Only the curlews are my companions; only the sound
> Of the wind in the bare birches can reach me through the wide air,
> Not the bleat of lambs, not the speech of man, not
> The gossiping of water, for the becks are frozen there.
> I gaze down on the larks, I gaze on the tops of the larches,
> I gaze into the long cleft of the dale, and see
> The dalefolk crawl like ticks in an old sheep's wool. (9)

The verse is also used to express urgently Elijah's doubts, his denunciations, forebodings, and prayers; and, when Ahab turns to verse, it is capable of pungent colloquialism:

> I've dug till my shoulders ache and there's not a drop
> Nor a hint of water in the bitter rocks—
> All as dry as a badger's backside. (46)

But the most interesting function of the verse, as it displays a fundamental aspect of the play's theme, is perhaps to be found early in Act III in a sequence of three speeches in which Martha, Ruth, and Obadiah describe to one another their experiences on Carmel Fell when Elijah prayed to God for a sign of His power. Apart from the speeches of the Beck, this sequence is the only purely lyrical use of verse in the play. Each speech begins with a variant of the same phrase, and this device gives the sequence something of the unity of a single poem. The imagery used by the three characters is derived from their ordinary experience of the natural world, but what they are gropingly trying to communicate by its use is a super-natural, spiritual experience:

> It was not what I saw,
> But what I heard. A great wind rose,
> Roaring down on the plain like a stormy sea
> Or a luggage train at a distance. Not a grass stirred
> Nor the dust moved on the rocks. There was no breeze
> On my brow, and my hair was as stiff as wire,
> But the wind whirled round me, screaming like a seagull,
> Whipped and herded like a pack of hounds—

> Yet a wisp of sheep's wool caught on the hooks of the crags
> Lay all the while still as a dog-whelk shell. (57)

The point is that Nicholson has given this extremely sensitive speech, and the two that follow it, not to Elijah but to three ordinary characters who usually express themselves in prose. The exchanging of prose for verse indicates their translation for a while to a different level of experience in which, without losing their identity, they come nearer to the divine meaning behind their existence. By choosing to express this pointed moment of awareness through the agency of everyday characters, Nicholson manages to suggest what the end of the play makes directly explicit—that it is in terms of limited human beings and day-to-day life that God makes Himself known in the world.

The Old Man of the Mountains has its faults. The influence of T.S. Eliot is rather too strongly present in the lines given to the Raven, who has a tendency to sound aloof and patronizing; and at times the play is too rawly didactic. The violent activity of Ahab early in Act III as he threatens to evict his tenants in order to build a dam creates a tension which, though superficially dramatic, is really a digression; and the rendering of the action on Carmel Fell by means of flashback (instead of by direct presentation as in the first version) blurs the play's generally straightforward following of the Bible narrative. But these objections are largely outweighed by the play's virtues—its ability to hold the attention and to communicate simply and strongly a sense of emotional concern. The suspense and the final triumph of the original story are forcefully recreated and given urgent contemporary relevance by Nicholson's awareness of the evils of uncontrolled materialism. The language of the play is vigorous, homely, humorous, and moving by turns; and the characters, through not subtle, are credibly human. It is easy to agree with Henry Reed's special commendation of Nicholson's protagonist: "His Elijah is a really dramatic character; the picture of him surrounded by his inspiration, his muddle, his faith and his pathetic self-doubting is particularly fine."[17]

Perhaps the most solid testimony to the effectiveness of the play is the many performances it has had. One of its reviewers was not being double-edged in his description when he said that "It is, unless we are being unduly optimistic, ideally a play for village domestic groups, and we can think of no better setting for it than the barns and greens of our English hamlets."[18]

[124]

The play has, in fact, been taken up by a wide variety of acting groups and has had at least twenty-four distinct presentations in very different places between 1945 and 1960, a respectable total for a verse play set in one particular area of England. There is a great deal to be said, and not by way of deprecation, for a play which has been performed before miners at Easington Colliery, County Durham, and to audiences in Croydon and Cheltenham; by pupils of two English grammar schools and by university students in New York; in the ruins of Coventry Cathedral; in Denmark; and in Christchurch, New Zealand.

II   Prophesy to the Wind

Published in 1950, Nicholson's second play, *Prophesy to the Wind,* is his only one with a theme apparently secular and with a plot of his own invention. It was commissioned in 1947 by the Little Theatre Guild which specified that it be "a play about a post-atomic age."[19] Nicholson's acceptance of such a commission suggests that he did not want just to be labelled "Christian dramatist" but wished to gain a reputation of a more diversified kind. A secular subject perhaps offered him a challenge to evolve a dramatic poetry unsupported by the overtones of biblical verse rhythm and an action which precluded the doctrinally conditioned response. It is certainly clear from a program note which Nicholson wrote for one of the performances of the play that he was stimulated and concerned by the implications for man's future of Hiroshima and Nagasaki—the problem of reconciling the need for scientific investigation with the need to control science's discoveries.

Prophesy to the Wind consists of a prologue and four scenes. The prologue establishes impressionistically, and indeed rather perfunctorily, the idea of an atomic cataclysm, out of which John, the industrial technician who represents the scientific attitudes of the contemporary world, is projected into the "future" of the play's four scenes. But the prologue does more than establish a context. As John is "whirled away with the draught/ Up the chimney of time," his urgent rhetorical question, "You who sit watching/ Am I not one of you?" invites the audience's immediate involvement and directs its attention to the possibility that the play is to be about it.

Nicholson deals with the problem of giving his hypothetical "future" at least the illusion of reality by making it a slighly distorted mirror image of the past. He shows post-atomic life as reverting to an already known, premechanistic culture—that of the Vikings who had originally taken possession of Cumberland. Much of the play's cultural framework and many of its allusions draw their life from customs and habits made familiar by the Icelandic sagas; and Nicholson's actual language is often reminiscent, both in choice of word and in turn of phrase, of translations of these. His decision to flesh the future on the bones of the past gives his characters a degree of solidity, but it carries the danger that at certain points—in some of the exchanges between Hallbjorn and Vikar, for instance—the play verges on historical costume drama and sounds archaic.

It is in this "neo-Viking" world that the rest of the play is acted out: in this simple community, the economic bases are embodied in Ulf, the sheep farmer, and his brother Hallbjorn, who digs and smelts iron to make the primitive plows, harrows, and scythes which he needs. As if aware of the danger that the audience may mistake the future for the past, Nicholson immediately makes it conscious of the distortions in the mirror image. Ulf enters carrying a mudguard, of whose purpose he is ignorant: "A rare big well-fleshed beast it must have been/ That took this blade to skin it" (9). His misunderstanding is also developed comically when he infers from it that "They were a race of giants in those days. . . ." The irony of this statement is underlined by a comment from Freya that six lambs will not go far among her cousin Vikar and his five companions who are soon expected to arrive: the humorous implied comparison would not have been wasted on an audience living in postwar austerity Britain. Another echo of the past comes when Vikar arrives (14) wearing an air raid warden's helmet which he has found in some ruins. The initial effect of both mudguard and helmet is to create, in the context, a comic incongruity; but not far beneath lurks the implication that the "race of giants" could not save itself from destruction. It is, however, in a haunting description by Hallbjorn of the ruins of the former world that the play's warning is really given:

> . . . when you venture inland,
> As I did, moving south, in search of tin,
> You come across a country where the land
> Is dead as slag or cinders. Not even a rat
> Lives there; a worm, a snake; not even a bird flies over.
> The dust stings the eyes. Drink of the gulleys
> And soon you'll vomit rotten flesh and maggots

And die within the hour. . . .
This is the land of the people who once were great
And now— (23)

From brooding on these evidences of disaster, Hallbjorn has evolved a
quietist view of life in which "Wealth, power, pride, and even honour/
Are dangers in the dale," and he therefore insists that Vikar, if he
wishes to marry his daughter Freya, must give up his life of piracy and
settle down.

Into this world, dominated by the "immovable object" which is
Hallbjorn's pastoral conservatism—a conservatism depicted as noble, the
fruit of sensitivity and thought, rather than stagnant and
cowardly—suddenly bursts John, still in a state of shock, speaking the
same short-lined verse (akin to that of "Silecroft Shore") as in the
prologue, describing the cataclysm and, as before, involving the
audience in his predicament. Scene II shows John and Freya, who
nurses him, falling in love as they talk of the two different worlds to
which they are accustomed. Behind John's description, of what is
recognizably Nicholson's own area, can be inferred one of the
imaginative impulses of the play: the side-by-side existence of the
derelict Hodbarrow Mines and the activity of Millom ironworks
probably prompted Nicholson to imagine a world in which the possible
consequences of man's search for knowledge and power were acted out.
The most significant event in the scene is John's discovery of an old
dynamo, which re-arouses in him the "irresistible force" of the
scientific impulse: "This/ Is the heart of my dead world, ready to beat/
When I put my fingers to the valves" (40).

In Scene III John and Hallbjorn finally arrive at the collision which
their opposite views of life make inevitable. Hallbjorn's shock on
discovering Freya's wish to marry John provokes John to demonstrate
his powers by making the dynamo work to turn a wheel. When
Hallbjorn realizes that the dynamo's power may ultimately lead to the
re-creation of a world which has already destroyed itself once, his
reaction is instinctive and hostile:

Destruction, boy,
Lies like disease in man's blood. When he is alone
And the air blows through his lungs, his breath is wholesome;
But when he stews and stinks in herds, plague
Breeds in his bones and blights them.

[127]

> But here it shall not come. Here in this dale
> Man shall retain something of his true health—Go,
> Break up your machine. (61)

This John cannot do; his scientific pursuits are "mine to deny no more/ Than I can deny the need to breathe." Fearing that John will be "a. frond/ Of burning bracken thrown in a dry pinewood," Hallbjorn sends him to Vikar with a dagger, whose purpose John, with a rather implausible innocence, does not see. Vikar, in the fashion of the Icelandic sagas, understands the tacit message and kills John offstage.

Plainly the play cannot end here. Though Hallbjorn's reasons for resisting scientific knowledge have been demonstrated as sincere and understandable, his action in having John killed too brutally upsets the balance created by the equal weights of the arguments presented and produces the expectation that the tension will be resolved in some less negative way. Despite their differences, there is too much in common between Hallbjorn's statement—"Man/ Is rock made mortal, and within the rock/ He finds his immortality"—and John's description of himself as one for whom "The slow geological/ Chemistry is my craft and study" (53) for the audience to think of Hallbjorn's action as anything but a false step. Though Hallbjorn's *volte-face* into recriminations against Vikar is a well-worn dramatic device, it is not insincere: Hallbjorn, presented all along as a good man, at once sees his ill-judged haste as a betrayal of his integrity:

> [I] came to this dale seeking a practical peace,
> A not-yet mortgaged conscience.
> And now I have thrown away my right. . .
> To save blood I've shed blood.

After Hallbjorn's feeble ashamed efforts to hide the truth from Freya, the resolution of the play's dialectical conflict unexpectedly yet credibly arrives in human terms: Freya is pregnant with John's child. As if to demonstrate that he is not created in the stereotyped, dishonor-avenging image of the Viking, Hallbjorn accepts the unborn child as a person when he would not accept his father as a theorist. Too late for John, he achieves a more open view of the future; he is prepared to contemplate the possibility that the child will

> . . .have his father's skill, his curiosity,
> Trying his key in all the world's locks. Mebbe
> He'll find the click of that machine out yonder
> We've not yet broken up? (76)

The play ends with a return to the meter of the prologue as Freya addresses the audience, laying on it the moral responsibility for what the future will be:

> Yes, you are here,
> You to whom John belonged,
> To whom he spoke, you
> To whom he has returned,
> What do you send for his son?

To resolve the play's problem by means of a child, though trite and rather too convenient, is not so sentimental as it may appear. It is hard to see how the tension between the protagonists' equal impulses—the one, to fear; the other, to hurry after potentially destructive but also potentially beneficial scientific knowledge—could have been satisfactorily resolved except by some such introduction of a third party. The introduction specifically of a child is of particular value to the play's emotional impact since it enables the play to end, not with the dry abstraction of such a phrase as "the human quest for knowledge should not be stamped out," but with the more deeply human feeling that an unborn child should not be killed.

Although *Prophesy to the Wind* has been classified as an apparently secular play, and although Nicholson has chosen not to bring in explicit religious values, its theme—the proper use of power—is sufficiently close to that of *The Old Man of the Mountains* to imply an ultimately religious attitude behind it. Hallbjorn, with his distrust of wealth and what may be considered as his noble conservatism, has a strength reminiscent of Elijah's in his more confident moments. He resembles Elijah also in his final recognition that science is not necessarily something to be resisted. Moreover, there are certainly times when John sounds like a more innocent version of Ahab:

> I'll break off flakes of sun, blue cracks of sky
> And hang them in the lobbies of dark woods;
> I'll make black metal burn, and falling water
> Lift ten-ton rocks like billiard-balls.
> I'll bring wealth to the dale. (41)

The use of John, at the beginning, and Freya, at the end, as fingers pointing at the audience is akin to the sermonizing habit of the Raven.

[129]

Most of all, the play's biblical title suggests the larger religious context in which the play belongs: "Then said he unto me, Prophesy unto the wind, prophesy, son of man, and say to the wind, Thus saith the Lord God; come from the four winds, O breath, and breathe upon these slain, that they may live" (Ezekiel xxvii, 9). On one level, the reference to Ezekiel indicates Nicholson's own bringing alive, in his play, of a ruined civilization; on another, it describes the play's action: "these slain" refers to the dead civilization, both buildings and people, of the postwar atomic age; and the "wind" is John's re-animation of the dynamo which can bring back their life. But, on yet another level, the passage surely suggests the nature of the future, which is left in doubt at the end of the play: a future in which, with an awareness of God, the past knowledge and civilization may return but be properly organized and controlled.

By creating a fable, instead of using a biblical story in which Divine intervention is possible, Nicholson has produced a play which is more strictly dramatic, more open-ended, than *The Old Man of the Mountains*. The plot allows more scope for argument and for the free interplay of ideas; and, because the ending of *Prophesy to the Wind* is not laid down in advance by any source, Nicholson has a better opportunity to surprise the audience by his resolution of the play's conflict. T. S. Eliot called the play "a real technical advance,"[20] and Nicholson's own impression of the play's performance in Ealing in 1949 suggests that its conclusion was particularly successful in practice: "This element of surprise—the sudden reversal of fortune, the complete new landscape of significance, which arises in the last act, does most certainly make the play end much more effectively than *The Old Man*."[21]

The play also resembles its predecessor in employing both verse and prose, but its argument is more closely knit and the amount of prose is smaller. The same pattern, however, obtains for its use—the prose passages express moments of lower intensity, but they are not spoken exclusively by certain characters. The verse of the play (leaving aside the short, stabbing lines used in the prologue to indicate the present, or by John to suggest his sense of strangeness on arriving in the future, or by Freya at the end to identify herself symbolically with John) fluctuates between iambic pentameters and alliterative lines which resemble those of the poem "Caedmon" in *Rock Face* and emphasize, as in this swashbuckling speech of Vikar's, the play's "Norse" setting:

> For years
> I ferreted the northern firths;
> Foraged and fratched and foundered, and all I brought
> Home were wounds and a story. . . .
> So I said goodbye to the midnight ice,
> Turned to the Hebrides and the Celtic lochs,
> And found five Irishmen with heads as fiery
> As any volcano in the vaults of Iceland,
> No more bankrupt buccaneering now—
> My Irishmen can save me all that trouble.
> They can lead to the door that's lightly latched,
> The village worth a visit. (18)

Prophesy to the Wind was first performed at the Newcastle People's Theatre in January, 1949, and again, three months later, at the Questors Theatre, Ealing. The play was vital enough on the stage to provoke T. S. Eliot, on leaving the theater after the Ealing performance, to remark that Nicholson "ought to be a very happy man."[22] Reviews of the play as published in 1950 were, on the whole, favorable; but a review of the Ealing production suggested a significant weakness in its occasional fluctuations of style. These result partly from the plot, where a modern character is placed in a pseudo-Viking context, so that two kinds of language are spoken. So much may have been dramatically inevitable, but there are less excusable blemishes which could easily have been removed. Such a one is John's speech to Hallbjorn where he says of the dynamo: "This is the brand, the strawberry-shaped birthmark/ To prove me legitimate to the rock" (53). The impression this statement gives is of the confusion of Shakespeare and Victorian melodrama of mistaken identity, and the use of "strawberry-shaped birthmark" as a metaphor shows an extreme lack of artistic tact, seeming more of a private joke to the audience than a reference which Hallbjorn would be likely to understand. Vikar's jealousy of John's courtship of Freya is expressed in a Shakespearean simile whose lazy borrowing suggests lack of interest on Nicholson's part: "Have I not watched them, their heads together/ Like two cherries on one stalk?" (46).[23] When the dynamo will not start, John attributes its failure to "a faulty circuit only" (56)—an inversion for which no reason is apparent, especially as it occurs in a short passage of prose. When Vikar defends his killing of John (70), he uses the pointless abbreviation "heritance" instead of the normal word. These instances and others combine to suggest a basic uncertainty in the use of language from which *The Old Man of the Mountains* does not suffer.

Stylistic maladroitness is accompanied by uncertainty in the handling of dramatic tone or level. Though the play deals with a serious theme, total acceptance of it is blurred by Nicholson's excursions into comedy. The flirtations of the servants Dick and Bessie, Freya's early "woman's-magazine" emphasis on the hypothetical "girls" in John's former life, and her immediate and immature desire to marry him, though they help the audience to believe in the "humanity" of these characters from the future, do so in a way unsuitably reminiscent of provincial domestic manners and thus detract irritatingly from the force of the main theme. Although Vikar, as the agent of Hallbjorn's mistake, is dramatically necessary, the stress on the "unheroic" aspects of his personality—his seasickness, his preference of whisky to wine—is an irrelevant amusement, indulged in to the detriment of the play as a whole. His gift to Freya of a ring with "part of the finger still inside it" (19) is Jacobean drama cheaply parodied, and his final exit line—"Therefore, Cousin,/Farewell" (76)—is pure melodrama. The various lapses diminish as the conflict gathers momentum, but they seriously mar a play whose very plot has a second-hand quality which may limit the audience's involvement.

In July, 1951, after hearing that the play was to be produced at the Watergate Theatre in London, Nicholson commented enigmatically in a letter that "I feel curiously uninterested, as if, in some way, I didn't quite own the play."[24] Nicholson's detachment suggests a degree of disenchantment, perhaps a feeling that the play, successful or otherwise, was not truly characteristic of his work. Any disenchantment was certainly deepened by the critical response to its performance at the Watergate in August, 1951. Even a fairly favorable review spoke of the play's being "less effective on the stage than it was on the printed page,"[25] while the *Observer,* although it admitted "many flashes of fine poetry," considered the plot "clumsily contrived" and likely to do "the cause of today's poetic drama little service."[26] Despite apparently being prepared for such reactions,[27] Nicholson was very much disappointed, saying in a letter that "I can't but be more and more aware of the gap between what I have to give and what even the most sympathetic expect."[28]

Considering that, in itself and in the total response it provoked, *Prophesy to the Wind* was by no means a complete failure, Nicholson's feelings seem to have been unduly depressed. The Little Theatre Guild, the commissioner of the play, spoke of having enjoyed it "better than any...they have done in the whole ten years of their existence;[29] but this testimonial does not seem to have compensated for its lack of metropolitan success. Nicholson's later plays returned to specifically religious subjects, and his abortive venture into secular drama remained a case by itself.

III   A Match for the Devil

Nicholson's third play, *A Match for the Devil* (1955), is difficult to judge objectively. The circumstances surrounding its composition and production were so unfortunate that any criticism of the play itself is mitigated by sympathy for its author, who seems throughout to have been between two stools. Having written his play for one kind of audience, Nicholson found it exposed to another; having disappointed the theological expectations of the play's commissioners, Nicholson was unable to satisfy the artistic requirements of the London critics. The result was "a fair notion fatally injured," but it was so injured as much by outside pressures as by its own internal flaws. Hence a description of it verges on an account of the tribulations of the Christian dramatist.

Nicholson began to tinker with what gradually turned into *A Match for the Devil* in the summer of 1951, having been greatly stimulated by his recent reading of the Book of Hosea. In March, 1952, E. Martin Browne requested from him, on behalf of the Religious Drama Society, something "for a new company of touring professionals—something like the Pilgrims—who are to be formed by Pamela Keily."[30] Nicholson saw in the group, which was to cater to church audiences in the larger industrial towns, just the right vehicle for the sort of play he envisaged. He had been given to understand that its audiences would not be narrow-mindedly "churchy," and his treatment in the finished play of the theme of sacred prostitution was based on this assumption. At the time the play was commissioned, Nicholson had decided its title and its verse form, which he described as a "cadenced metre."[31] He had also decided to set the play in Palestine rather than in Cumberland and to treat his material loosely and anachronistically—"a kind of charade treatment" in which Hosea would keep "something like a little baker's shop, with customers and a... suggestion of counter etc."[32] The material itself, however, underwent many changes before Nicholson finally submitted an outline of the play to the New Pilgrims in May, 1952, and completed the first three scenes—to the satisfaction of Browne and Pamela Keily—in June.

The New Pilgrims put the play into rehearsal, but early in 1953 came a totally unexpected setback. The Religious Drama Society intervened and "gave orders to stop production."[33] This dictatorial prejudgment ruined the play's chances of the kind of performance Nicholson had had in mind when writing it, and in part gave rise to his difficulties later. The Society's reasons (with Browne, a director, a minority of one) were fourfold: ". . .the audience would object to the association of religion with prostitution. . .audiences will confuse the Temple with present-day churches;. . .the prophetic element is given to the Boy instead of Hosea, and. . .the play is a comedy instead of a Tragedy."[34] These objections were based on no more substantial a foundation than Nicholson's submitted outline of the play. Moreover, the objections reveal considerable moral narrowness, an unpleasant degree of condescension, and a wish to limit the dramatist's choice of approach to his material. Nicholson himself later explained something of this approach in his radio talk "The Comic Prophet" (1953).[35] However it should be noted here of the first complaint that the theme of sacred prostitution is treated without sensationalism and is entirely historical, for it is based on the picture presented in the Book of Hosea and the Book of Amos of the decline and corruption of the Jewish religion: ". . .and a man and his father will go in unto the same maid, to profane my holy name: And they lay themselves down upon clothes laid to pledge by every altar, and they drink the wine of the condemned in the house of their god" (Amos ii, 7–8).[36] All in all, the reaction of the Religious Drama Society, palliated by "not a word of regret, apology or gratitude,"[37] was a performance which, viewed from a secular standpoint, seems almost as ludicrous as it was discreditable.

It is worth recording the dismay which the New Pilgrims themselves felt when production was stopped: to them "the verdict came as a terrible blow."[38] The practical effect of the ban was to leave on Nicholson's hands a play "cut very closely to the requirements" of the New Pilgrims "and of the audiences they would meet."[39] It was a play better suited, he felt, for the provinces than for London because of its "small-town stall-shop atmosphere."[40] What must have seemed at the time the solution to Nicholson's problem was arrived at in July, 1953, when the play was adopted by the well-thought-of London Club

Theatre Group. It was decided to produce it during the Edinburgh Festival, and the first performance took place in St. Mary's Hall, Edinburgh, on August 28, 1953.

The theme of *A Match for the Devil*—love and reconciliation rather than law and denunciation—is taken from the Book of Hosea; and Nicholson's plot, better described as a kind of dramatic improvisation, is based on the narrative suggestion embedded in the mainly prophetic manner of its first three chapters. Chapter One presents Hosea's instruction from God to "take unto thee a wife of whoredoms" (v. 2) and tells how his marriage to Gomer produced three children; Chapter Two suggests her unfaithfulness to him but in language so unspecific that it refers as much to Israel and God as to Gomer and Hosea; and Chapter Three describes how Hosea was instructed to take back his unfaithful wife. The Bible text, however, seems more interested in Hosea's marriage as a metaphor of God's love for erring humanity than in its domestic details.

Nicholson is concerned, as he shows in Hosea's speech to Amos (48–49), to convey the Divine implications of Hosea's love for Gomer; but, as a dramatist, he is equally involved in showing the Bible's symbolic figures as human beings. He therefore invents a number of characters whose existence gives Hosea and Gomer a physical frame of reference. David, Gomer's "love-child" by a temple worshipper, takes the place of the three children of Hosea's marriage and acts also as the necessary intermediary in the play for God's messages to Hosea. Sarah, Rachel, Esther, and the Scribe are created to give Hosea's story a social context and to embody the ridicule to which as a cuckold he was presumably subjected; the High Priest Amaziah is imported from the Book of Amos to serve as an apologist for ritual prostitution; and the prophet Amos himself is introduced to give expression to harsher, disapproving attitudes in contrast with which the tolerance and forgiveness of Hosea can more easily be appreciated.

The play is entirely in verse. Two reasons may be advanced for this departure from Nicholson's usual practice. One is that the pseudo-Palestinian setting is amenable to a thoroughgoing use of verse, especially as Nicholson incorporates much biblical phrasing and imagery; also applicable is Eliot's point, made in *Poetry and Drama* (1951), that "picturesque period costume renders verse much more acceptable." The other reason lies in the play's fairly constant maintenance of a single tone—one of seriously intentioned "comedy"—rather than the mixture of high and low pressure, human and divine levels, ancient story and modern setting, which characterizes *The Old Man of the Mountains. A Match for the Devil* is the only play of Nicholson's which either intentionally follows, or is enabled by its single tone and setting to follow, Eliot's recommendation that "we should aim at a form of verse in which everything can be said that has to be said."[41] Nicholson's very flexible verse form is based on "the sense of backward and forward flowing, a balancing not of stress against stress but of the whole cadence of a sentence or phrase against another sentence."[42] It is influenced by the antiphonal patterning of the Psalms and also by Ezra Pound's *Cantos,* which Nicholson had been systematically reading through early in 1951; and it is able to modulate easily from ordinary conversational language into prophetic denunciation or colorful lyricism.

The ease of the verse is apparent in Hosea's self-introductory speech at the opening of the first scene. Hosea is presented as a baker, according to a tradition which derives from his fondness for images drawn from baking. This view of him and his direct address to the audience recall the down-to-earth manner of the Miracle Plays; indeed, the simplified motivations of the characters, together with the play's occasional employment of knockabout farce, link *A Match for the Devil* with the tradition of "ritual drama." The confidential tone adopted by Hosea epitomizes the attitude of moderation and tolerance which the play conveys:

> The name's Hosea—
> Baker and confectioner;
> Bread, cakes, scones fresh daily;
> Weddings and funerals catered for.
> I'm a stranger to this part of Jezreel
> And looking out for custom;
> Just give me a trial
> And I'll guarantee satisfaction.
> I come from the next-door-to country,
> From the plain of Megiddo—
> Under the juts of the town walls
> In the smother of the road to Samaria.
> I could stand in my orchard and look twelve miles one way to Mount Carmel,
> And twelve miles the other way to Mount Gilboa,

[136]

And the plain between like a full-tide sea with islands—
  Blue whirlpools of wheat frothing in the wind.
It was a place you could stretch your arms in.[43]

A later speech by Sarah, who runs an old clothes stall next to Hosea's
baker's shop, indicates neatly the secular decadence of the world in
which Hosea now finds himself, a world of "live now, pay later":

At night it's dimples on the draped divans,
Red wine spilt on the ivory,
  Yellow stains of sherbet embroidering the carpet.
But who's to find the money in the morning?
  Why, mother Sarah with her tick-and-try shop—
Any old damask, any old rubies—
  Any old thing at all that their husbands won't remember. (15)

Gomer, Sarah's daughter in the play, represents the religious
decadence of the period in which "ritual prostitution was tolerated
even in the temples of Yahweh,"[44] but the presentation of Gomer as a
temple prostitute is a complex one. She is seen by Rachel as no more
than "this cast-off comfort girl from the chapel of ease" (81); by her
mother, with salacious innuendo, as "a handmaid/ A maid very much to
hand" (17); and by Amos simply as a harlot. But Gomer sincerely sees
herself as performing a less purely sensual function: "True, desire
strikes like an apoplexy:/ Making the senses dizzy with greed—/ But yet
there is also a giving:—/ Under the hot nerves, in the cool of the heart,/
There is also a quiet giving. . . ./ To Yahweh" (20). Amaziah sees her as
merely different from "true" Jews: "Her blood is of the ancient race of
Canaan,/ Pagan as the stone circles of Gilgal" (69). Nicholson's
willingness to entertain serious views of Gomer may have affronted the
Religious Drama Society; however, because of these views, the play is
prevented from being a tract on the stock Victorian theme of the
reformation of a fallen woman.
    When Gomer appears in the first scene, she has become tired of the
"growing emptiness" of her profession and has left the temple at
Samaria. David, the son who is ignorant of what her "religious duties"
have involved, plans to marry her to Hosea, to whom he has attached
himself, and Gomer willingly accepts his plan. The process by which
David persuades Hosea, who is "as proud of being single as if he were
commander/ Of all King Jeroboam's chariots," to marry Gomer is

[137]

omitted, just as Hosea's reasons for obeying God's instructions are ignored by the Bible. The second scene simply presents him as married to Gomer and as happy, uxorious, and caring too much for her. Gomer wishes to be useful, to feel that she can "bring something" to the marriage; but Hosea's kindness unwittingly relegates her to the status of an ornament. When she asks him, "do I bring you nothing?,", his answer—too concerned with his own feeling of happiness—is not the reassurance that she seeks:

> No, dearest, you bring the flowers from nowhere,
> Holding them like a magician hidden in your sleeve;
> You swill the very flagstones with a bucketful of light.
> You wind up the finches and set the throstles working
> Till every bush twinkles like a musical box. (32)

When Gomer becomes bored with doing nothing, she disappears with the primary intention of getting Hosea the contract to bake bread for the temple. While she is away, Amos enters and denounces the sinfulness of Samaria in his own biblical words. Hosea interposes, with a moderation founded on his own happiness, a less harsh view of God's relation to man:

> . . .up on your limestone balcony,
> Hearing the wind relaying its messages,
>   You learn of the glory of Yahweh,
> The power of Yahweh,
>   The judgement of Yahweh,
> But never of the love of Yahweh.
>   We can learn more of that here in Jezreel. (47)

By a very effective dramatic irony, Hosea is talking in this strain just as Gomer, offstage, has succumbed to the attractions of the paganized temple of Jezreel. Sarah, who has been to look for her, reveals the true state of affairs in two harsh, superbly balanced lines which conclude the scene with a fine effect of shock:

> Gomer has returned to her former profession:
> Your wife is one of the temple prostitutes.

In the third scene, which takes place eight months later, Hosea's unhappiness is reflected in the little heart he now has for his baking, and the betrayal by his wife lays him open to the bitter influence of Amos. On page fifty-eight, he speaks in gloomy chorus with him, taking a significantly similar tone. But, for Hosea, Gomer is not the only harlot; her unfaithfulness symbolizes the backsliding of the country as a whole. His picture of this, lyrically painted as much in sorrow as in anger, presents the first of the three meanings of the play's title:

> This land of Israel is a land of harlots. . .
> This land that Yahweh took as wife,
> His chosen, his cherished one,
> Plaiting the wild vines in her hair,
> Looping her shoulders in a weave of lilies;
> This land that he held as a bridegroom holds his bride,
> Tacking the blue braid of the Jordan in the hem of her petticoat;
> And this land, this wife,
> Has turned away from her husband, away from Yahweh.
> She has become an adulteress.
> She has ogled after heathen lovers,
> She has become a mate for idols,
> A match for the devil. (57)

David, acting as the voice of God, suggests that Hosea should take Gomer back; but Hosea, unwilling to add to the ridicule of cuckoldry the humiliation of being a complaisant husband, refuses; and the scene ends with David, in a touch of visual symbolism rare in Nicholson's plays, dejectedly looking for the mouse, given him earlier by his mother, which he has lost.

Scene Four, however, shows Hosea at the temple, ready to forgive his wife; for he now believes in David's wisdom because of a dream he has had in which David appeared "all preened out as the Child Samuel" (64).[45] Hosea is represented as following the instructions of David, who has even told him what to say. He himself does not quite understand God's will for him and is not, in any case, sure that what he is seeking will come about: "But she left me of her own free-will;/ And of her own free-will why should she return?" (66). Here Hosea is pointing to the greatest difficulty which had confronted Nicholson when he was writing the play—that of providing a reason for Gomer's return to Hosea; "indeed," he said at the time in a letter, "I nearly gave up the play on account of it."[46]

Nicholson's solution of the problem imposed on him by the absence of motivation for Gomer's return in his biblical source, though it apparently worked when the play was performed, is not altogether convincing on paper; and the last scene is unfortunately the least satisfactory in the play. Its changes of direction are rather too rapid, giving the impression that it is working out a preconceived didactic pattern. Just as Gomer's action in leaving Hosea seems too abrupt, so does her initial response to his arrival at the temple seem too easy; and, when difficulties do arise over Hosea's forgiveness of her, which she finds patronizing and unacceptable, their solution on a comic level by David's ruse of appearing bedraggled and unsandaled, yet pretending to repudiate his and Hosea's need of her, seems a deliberate undermining of the serious issues which the play presents. It is David's trick which earns from Amaziah his sobriquet "a match for the devil."

One of the serious issues disappointingly sidestepped in the play is raised by Hosea's reaction to Gomer's anger at his "forgiveness." Hosea seems to accept Amaziah's view that Gomer is different and that—with the rather destructive proviso that she give up her occupation—her "difference" must be accepted:

HOSEA. I spoke of forgiving when I ought to have asked for forgiveness.
AMAZIAH. Forgiveness? And what for?
HOSEA (to Gomer) For wanting you not what you are;
    For offering you the consciousness of guilt in part-exhange for love.
    When I speak of sin, Amaziah, I distort her innocence;
    When I speak of forgiveness, I put her in the wrong. (79)

This reasoning leads Hosea into deeper waters; in probing into the nature of God's forgiveness, he seems to imply that Gomer's hostility to his own is understandable:

    But what does his forgiveness mean?
    It asks us to be what we don't want to be—
    We resent the presumption.
    We deny the right.
    How can God begin to forgive us
    Till we learn to forgive God?

At this point, Hosea is interrupted by David; and the play is steered quickly to its conclusion. Hosea is rambling on, and the interruption is dramatically necessary; but it seems also to serve the less admirable purpose of avoiding the unsuitably unorthodox conclusion to which Hosea's over-elliptical obscurities may be leading. Nicholson seems to shirk exploring the deeper implications which he suggests, and he thus leaves the reader feeling intellectually cheated.

Not quite convincingly, then, the play reaches the conclusion laid down by its source: Gomer returns to Hosea. In accepting Gomer for what she is (though the play's ambiguities of treatment do not really succeed in making "what she is" very clear), Hosea demonstrates the triumph of love over law, which the play's two epigraphs (Genesis iii, 15, and Romans xvi, 20) indicate as the final meaning of the play's title. Hosea's return to the joys of marriage is an assertion of the affirmative way in the face of the negative way represented by the isolationism of Amos. Public ridicule no longer matters, and Gomer and Hosea in their reconciliation prove that human love is "a match for the devil."

Nicholson once referred to *A Match for the Devil* as his "favourite among the plays."[47] It is clear from the many stages which the text went through before arriving at its final form that it is certainly a play on which Nicholson expended much effort. It is, in addition, unusual among his output in dealing not only with a religious theme but with the difficult real relationship between a man and a woman. Whether *A Match for the Devil* is considered successful, however, partly depends on how easily audience and reader can accept the "charade" treatment which Nicholson, writing originally for church audiences in industrial towns, adopted for his subject. Though the three main characters—Hosea, Gomer, and David—are lovingly brought to life, the minor characters, Amaziah excepted, are little more than stock figures who introduce into the play an air of bustle and often of farce which, while lively and amusing, reduce the seriousness of the theme. The use of such elements may perhaps be defended on the practical grounds that Nicholson needed to interest the amateur groups and local audiences at which he aimed, but they are less easy to accept on the printed page.

Nor is Nicholson's "charade" treatment, involving "plenty of anachronism and no attempt at historical accuracy,"[48] maintained throughout the play. His concern about where the action should be located is attested by his consultation of the Old Testament scholar

Professor H. H. Rowley;[49] and Jezreel was chosen only after much careful sifting of other possibilities. This concern, together with Nicholson's attempt to establish, by quotation from the books of Amos and Hosea and of the Song of Solomon, an Old Testament atmosphere in his poetic language, suggests a wish to create some degree of verisimilitude. Reference to biblical place names and events, and the use of Amaziah, a sophisticated, slightly Eliotesque character of some dignity, to hint at the possible spiritual aspects of ritual prostitution bring into the play an illusion of historical realism. Thus critical standards need to keep changing in order to cope with a manner of presentation for which the basic criterion seems never to have been quite decided. Even Nicholson's use of "biblical" language—evident in its least serious form in Esther's exclamatory use of quotations like "Quicken me with quinces" and "Purge me with hyssop"—is not always consistent. Hosea himself sometimes speaks with a Cumbrian "naturalness," using dialect words like "lish" and "giversome" which are out of place in the Palestinian setting. A jarring example of incongruity is the Scribe's annoyance at the appearance of Hosea and David at the temple: "The rituals of the temple are not to be interrupted/ For the sake of every lout of the lonnings."[50]

The total effect of *A Match for the Devil* is thus difficult to assess. It is enjoyable, even at times delightful; and the verse has often an exhilarating freshness; but the play's success is at a fairly low level of emotional intensity. Of all its critics, Anne Ridler made the most acute observation when she wrote that "Mr. Nicholson has in this play deliberately subdued his talent."[51] Had Nicholson been aware from the start of the kind of critical climate to which his play would actually be exposed—instead of imagining an audience which the strictures of the Religious Drama Society prevented it from reaching—he might well have replaced some of its broader comic touches with a more searching development of the serious potentialities of his subject.

Nicholson went with some trepidation to the Edinburgh performance in 1953, wondering "whether the critics will take to what they usually feel is so *provincial* a point of view,"[52] The play was in fact successful with its audience, a predominantly Scottish one which included a number of distinguished Scots writers, among them the poet Hugh MacDiarmid. This audience, once it had "got hold of the idea of sacred prostitution," "followed the story intently."[53] Scottish and provincial English reviews of the play were approving, and a number of visiting students from Denison University, Ohio, liked the play well enough to stage it in their university theater later in the year.

Performance during the Edinburgh Festival carried with it, however, what was in this instance the double-edged privilege of exposure to the London critics. Their response was far from favorable: the play was charged with ineptitude, looseness of dramatic construction, too obvious a didactic intention, superficiality, and diffuseness. Harold Hobson, in *The Sunday Times,* was particularly curt and dismissive: "...my own tepid enthusiasm for the play is due, not to its morals, which seem to me impeccable, but to its dullness, to its wilderness of semi-Biblical metaphors, and its apparent belief that alliterations like 'Quicken me with quinces' are witty"[54] A similar reaction came from the *Church of England Newspaper* which, rather ironically, also made no mention of the theological drawbacks which had so sharply worried the Religious Drama Society: "The influence of Christopher Fry's early plays is apparent in the language, without Mr. Fry's subtle ambiguity. The language is altogether too lush; simply to reproduce the most exotic words in the Old Testament is not to produce poetry...."[55] Through many speeches in the play do bear a fortuitous general likeness to Fry's manner, Nicholson had never been one of his admirers and was trying simply "to suggest the poetical parts of the Old Testament prophets."[56]

Nicholson was very much disappointed with the reception of his play by the London critics, partly for practical reasons. He wrote to George Every that their reviews "seem to have put paid to any further productions of the play."[57] In view of the fact, however, that the Edinburgh audience and a number of non London papers had liked *A Match for the Devil,* Nicholson's statement, later in the same letter, that "this is the end of me as a dramatist," sounds excessive; for it was not London critics whom the play was originally designed to please.

The explanation for this apparent one-sidedness in Nicholson's feelings seems clear enough. A dramatist can conceive a play with one kind of audience in mind and yet still hope that it may succeed in a quite different atmosphere. It is easy to imagine how, after the intervention of the Religious Drama Society had ruined the prospect of performances by the New Pilgrims, the chance of a performance at the Edinburgh Festival could have created in Nicholson's mind the possibility that the play might win over the London critics and so perhaps bring about for him a breakthrough into the commercial theater. This hypothesis is supported by something Nicholson said later in a letter to Professor William Brasmer, who produced the play in America: "Of course, one would always like a metropolitan production and a financial success."[58]

While at the Edinburgh Festival, Nicholson attended the premiere (before a "fashionable, London type of audience") of Eliot's *The Confidential Clerk.* This experience seems to have indicated to him the gulf which stretched between what he had to offer and what sophisticated theatergoers wanted. For them, apparently, Eliot's conveyance of his spiritual meaning in the vehicle of drawing-room comedy was far more acceptable than Nicholson's way of presenting religious themes. It seemed that, to them, urbanely spoken characters like Sir Claude Mulhammer and Colby Simpkins were far more real than Hosea or, for that matter, Elijah. Such impressions must have combined with the hostile criticism of his own play to produce in Nicholson a conviction that the commercial theater was not for him, for his fourth play, *Birth by Drowning,* represents a return to the kind of pastoral morality with which he had begun his dramatic career.

IV   Birth by Drowning

All Nicholson's plays were written with a specific type of audience in mind, but *Birth by Drowning* (1960) is the only one which was also written for a particular occasion. The play was commissioned in 1957 by the Committee for Religious Drama in the Northern Province, whose adviser was Pamela Keily; and the occasion was the Commemoration Festivities of the Community of the Resurrection, based at Mirfield in Yorkshire. These festivities necessitated "a play which [could] be enjoyed by some 3 to 4 thousand folk of 'bank-holiday' texture."[59] The first draft was completed in March, 1959; and the play was performed, by a cast of theological students, in the open-air Quarry Theatre at Mirfield on July 9, 1959.

Much of the play's character can be immediately understood in terms of these practical circumstances. A religious occasion naturally called for a religious subject, and the fact that the play's audience would be composed predominantly of Northerners made its Cumbrian setting virtually inevitable for Nicholson. The great size of the audience—together with the fact that Pamela Keily was directing a cast of amateurs—also made necessary a play which would be fairly humorous in tone, simple in outline, and free of too many nuances of characterization. That the play begins with inanimate "characters"—the Three Fells—who call to one another and that it ends with the echoes of their messages become especially meaningful given the acoustics of outdoor performance; for the Fells' "larger-than-life" effect is appropriate to an open-air theater. In such a theater, employing few scenic props, the Fells serve a purpose comparable to that of a Greek chorus: they comment on the action (which they also "move . . .from place to place without any break in the dialogue"[60]); they anticipate the entry of some of the human characters; they indicate the passage of time; and they also, like the Raven in *The Old Man of the Mountains,* describe the physical scene and embody God's instructions to his prophet.

In the sense that the play deals with Elijah's successor, Elisha, *Birth by Drowning* may be thought of as a sequel to *The Old Man of the Mountains.* Like Nicholson's first play, his fourth deals with Old Testament events but transfers them to a Cumberland setting: the names and places remain biblical, but the rendering of events is almost entirely in modern terms—"almost," because the story of Elisha, like that of Elijah, contains miracles; and no attempt is made either to leave them out or to rationalize them. *Birth by Drowning* also resembles Nicholson's first play in employing almost as much prose as verse, and the action likewise fluctuates between ordinary conversation and passages of more pointedly thematic content.

These similarities, however, are surface matters only. Whereas *The Old Man of the Mountains* presents a deeply felt conflict, its "sequel" rarely involves the emotions; it resembles, therefore, a spectacle rather than a sermon. Elijah is a character movingly presented from the inside; Elisha is drawn altogether more broadly, a near-stereotype of a country doctor with a brisk, blunt, and homely manner. Compared, in fact, with all three of Nicholson's earlier plays, *Birth by Drowning* is an obviously lightweight effort which belies any complexities suggested by its paradoxical title.[61] To be lightweight, however, is not necessarily to be a failure. Its ill-fated predecessor, *A Match for the Devil,* seems ultimately to fail because its occasional notes of genuine anguish and its tantalizing hints at unexplored issues prompt a reader (if not a member of an audience) to judge it by stringent standards. *Birth by Drowning* raises no expectations of profundity and therefore tends to disarm criticism. A review of the play in the *Church Times* which commented on its "vigorous verse. . .study dialogue. . .[and] homely humour"[62] seems more pertinently geared to its quality than one in *The Times Literary Supplement* which concluded severely that "It would be a difficult moment for anyone arguing the cause of a serious theatre in which poets, if they were dramatists, could take part if they were confronted with this play."[63]

The key incident in the play, as its title indicates, is the healing of Naaman by Elisha described in II Kings v; but, since this episode is not introduced until Act III, the play as a whole actually represents the weaving together of a number of incidents and occasions in the Second Book of Kings. Nicholson treats his source material very freely not only in an obvious way by giving it a contemporary feeling but by rearranging it in an order of his own. The biblical material is, in fact, presented by the play in reverse order.

Act I deals with the return to Shunem Farm of its occupants (called Samuel and Miriam by Nicholson) after the seven year drought prophesied by Elisha in II Kings viii, 1—6. They bring with them the son whom Elisha had restored to life in II Kings iv, 35; he is given the name Gehazi, and he becomes Elisha's apprentice, both medically and spiritually. This first act takes place in an atmosphere of "Border Raids" which recall the medieval history of Cumberland as a debatable land between England and the Scots, but the biblical source for this atmosphere is the constant friction between Syria and Israel, and the two scenes of Act II dramatize its culmination in the King of Syria's attempt, described in II Kings vi, to abduct Elisha. As in the Bible, Elisha is saved by divine intervention, and in Scene I this incident is given a Cumbrian context:

ELISHA. Look at the fell-top.
    Look at the mist that hangs there
  As if that crag, crashing five hundred feet,
    Were a waterfall splashing spray in the air.
  Look at the sun,
    Quick as a trout, there, swimming in the mist.
  See it twisting as the wind swivels the current:
    See it diddering in the ripples of the vapour.
  There, Gehazi, stare straight into the glare of the sun.
    What do you see?
GEHAZI. Horses! White horses and chariots of fire:
  The sky alive with horses.

[146]

In Scene II, the Fells themselves save Elisha from capture and Dothan Dale, his home, from infiltration by intruding, in charade fashion, on the action; they blindfold Naaman and the Lieutenant with grayish muslin scarves to symbolize mountain mist and, in a version of "Oranges and Lemons," lead them astray until they are back in their own country, Borderland, again:

> Chase and chastise 'em
> Say the winds of Gerizim.
> Bend your backs lower
> Say the tracks of Gilboa.
> Shin up the steeple
> Say the crags of Mount Ebal.
> . . . . .
> Here comes a raven to peck out your eyes;
> And here comes a whirlwind to blow a SURPRISE.

During this "nursery rhyme" speech, Elisha himself helps to lead the "Bordermen" astray; and, when the scene ends, the humiliated Naaman understands that he has this "stranger" to thank for not having been handed over to his opposite number, General Joram.

Act III deals with the material presented in II Kings v. Naaman comes to Elisha, not knowing his connection with the previous incidents, to be cured of his leprosy. Realizing when he sees him that Elisha is the former enemy to whom he is already in debt, Naaman is more reluctant to accept a cure from him. In addition to the cure's being something which it is an effort for Naaman to swallow, it is a surprise to Elisha himself—and even more of a kindness on his part. Early in Act III, the Fells have warned him to prepare to cure an unknown patient; but, because he is too local in his loyalties, he does not connect the remedy they suggest ("Tell him to go and wash himself in the beck") with Naaman, the ex-enemy soldier; in Elisha's view, "The echoes speak only for those who belong to the dale" (56). Eventually, he realizes that "the echoes" are asking him to extend his own horizons, and he sees that Naaman is "the first man from beyond the bounds of the dale/ That the echoes ever spoke for" (58).

Nicholson's reversal of the biblical order of events throughout the play can thus be seen as a desire not only to put into meaningful sequence what seems in the Bible an episodic presentation of incidents but also to give the play a theme: in human terms, the need to forgive one's enemies; in political terms, the need to transcend the limitations of a parochial outlook. This theme is explicitly stated near the end of the play in a speech by Elisha:

> For we have learned
> That the Lord speaks not just to this dale
> But to the broad world. The echoes sound
> Far beyond the bounds of these mountains,
> And "Bordermen" and "foreigner" and "enemy"
> Are words that have no meaning any more. (62)

The view expressed by Elisha has great significance for Nicholson, himself as a provincial writer aware of the dangers of provincialism, but it would be wrong to imply that it predominates throughout the play, except in so far as the "Border" disharmony in which the various incidents take place requires some sort of resolution. Elisha's words have the baldness of an abstract summary, and their seriousness is not adequately prepared for by the play's earlier mixture of comedy, rustic realism, and charade. The actual curing of Naaman—rather than the moral which is drawn from it—is presented farcically, with the "twin Pikes" holding a ewer and a basin and splashing Naaman with water in a symbolic, parodic baptism. The end of the play swerves into an inappropriate repetition of the conclusion of *The Old Man of the Mountains,* with Elisha deploring the way in which the dales folk have apparently missed the spiritual point of the cure—God's message of brotherhood—and with his deciding to "climb to the high crags: I'll converse with the echoes/ When the fell wind blows strong." This reaction does not suit Elisha, who has not been presented as an insecure prophet, alternately trusted and derided by the people among whom he lives, but as a much more downright, simple character. It is only proper that the Fells, echoing the final words of his lines, should think his decision "wrong" and recall him to his true duty—"to hear for those who have no ears." The antiphonal last lines seem to pull the Third Act's loose ends almost forcibly together, with a buoyancy in keeping with the uncomplicated, largely light-hearted manner of the play as a whole:

ELISHA. Then let the long dale accept the weather of blessing.
THE THREE FELLS. And let every wind in the world blow praises to the Lord.

[148]

The essentially functional prose of the play, its syntax strongly tinged with dialectal inflections and its subject matter pungently conveying a rustic setting, needs no discussion. Its unambitious homeliness is well illustrated by a speech of Samuel's: "We'll just about be in time for the late ploughing. The land should be in right good heart after seven years' fallow, and with a scaling of muck on the meadows they'll think it's their birthday" (14). The verse is much more interesting, but it also is workmanlike rather than imaginative or emotionally intense. The human characters use a kind of verse which resembles that of *A Match for the Devil,* consisting of an approximate alternation of longer and shorter unrhymed lines. Though individual lines are colloquial in rhythm, the total effect is of a quiet but definite patterning of stresses which has its unconscious effect on the ear:

(ELISHA)	But I can tell you nowt. For weeks
	The fells have been empty of all echoes.
	Not even the thunder seems to rouse them.
	I've shouted and shouted,
	Chucked my voice against those crags—
	But it's like spitting into cotton wool. (27)

The verse given to the Fells is based on the same system of alternation, but ingenious end rhyme is added to create an effect of choral stylization and very frequently of comedy. Most of the colorful poetry in *Birth by Drowning* is spoken by the Fells. For all their homeliness, they open the play with a description which is clear and arresting:

GERIZIM.	What's the weather like at your end of the dale?
GILBOA.	A beautiful morning, Mount Gerizim: a pale
	Green mist lifting up from the sea like a venetian blind,
	And the wind
	Soap-sudding all the doorsteps of the shingle.

Much of the writing for the Fells, especially when seen on the page, has a decidedly virtuoso air. If the reader is not hampered, as the reviewer in *The Times Literary Supplement* was, by thinking them "basically ludicrous," he should enjoy, and be able to admire, the ingenuity Nicholson brings to their speeches. He wrote to George Every that

[149]

"[the Fells'] most 'poetic' images are often presented in deliberately comic language. I enjoyed myself enormously when I wrote their lines."[64] The comedy is theatrically most apparent in their various charade performances when they intervene to assist the action, but it can be appreciated equally well in the published play in their versification, with its skillful and often unlikely rhyming, as when Gilboa describes her neglected state after the seven-year drought:

And here, in the dale bottom, I'm up to the shins in mud; bogged
    And water-logged;
My hair's turning to peat, and fool's celery's cluttering up my gullies.
    I've knitted woollies
Out of every scrap of bog-cotton I could rake together. But there's
    nowt like a static
    Dyke-drain for aggravating my sciatica.
Ever since Samuel left Shunem farm
    My left arm
Flank has been sorely neglected.

The conception of the Fells themselves is the most striking aspect of the play, and they serve so many purposes that it is impossible to imagine the play without them. From their great height they enable the "Border" situation to be seen from both sides, as none of the individual characters could see it; and, in their unassuming way, they give the play's human action both a natural and a divine background. Their names—Gilboa, Ebal, and Gerizim—make clear the play's historical location in the plains and mountain passes of Northern Samaria,[65] but by calling Gilboa "Great Gilboa," and Ebal and Gerizim "the twin pikes" Nicholson is easily able to suggest a Cumberland setting: their similarity to Great Gable, Scafell, and Scafell Pike is obvious. It may be said that on the audience's ability to accept the humanization of the Fells—as gossipy, cross-talking, middle-aged housewives—depends its ability to enjoy the play.

A lengthier treatment of *Birth by Drowning* would suggest for it a quite false position of importance among Nicholson's plays. To attack its mixture of naturalistic dialogue and simple expressionism would be deliberately to miss its point, and to sneer at its unsubtle humor would be nearer to literary snobbery than to literary criticism. *Birth by Drowning* is a play which aims low, and any relevant final judgment must consider this fact. It pleased its audience—of the " 'parish party' type"[66]—both at Mirfield and at the performances which Pamela Keily subsequently directed in Manchester and in Sheffield. Thus, in its limited way, it fulfilled the limited purpose for which it was conceived.

V *Nicholson the Dramatist*

Birth by Drowning reveals with a special emphasis something shared by all Nicholson's plays: an essentially practical intention. Without venturing into the debatable land of "play as theater" versus "play as printed book," it seems reasonable to say that Nicholson's plays were intended to be acted rather than read, to be used and heard rather than pored over and analyzed. All of them were commissioned, and it is doubtful whether they would otherwise have been written. Without denigrating his plays, one may call Nicholson not a playwright by primary vocation, one who turned to drama as his inevitable means of expression, but a poet who has adopted dramatic form as a way of bodying-forth his religious concerns and gaining for them a more immediate and tangible public response than poetry by itself would have allowed.

Nicholson's plays form part of a twentieth-century literary-historical phenomenon: the revival of Christian verse drama. When Nicholson began his first play, verse seemed to promise the theater an injection of new vitality; and the attempt to present Christian themes on the stage was one which critics were disposed to take seriously. In 1944, E. Martin Browne felt able to declare that "the religious drama is fuller of life. . .than ever before. It has won the respect of the theatre as well as of the Church. . . Any religious play of the first rank could now emulate the success of *Murder in the Cathedral.*"[67] When Browne's season of "Plays by Poets" opened in 1945 at the Mercury Theatre, it attracted considerable attention in the national press. Thus Nicholson made his theatrical debut in a very favorable atmosphere. By the end of the next decade, the situation was very different. When Nicholson's fourth play was produced in 1959, both verse and Christianity had lost their preeminence in drama. Since John Osborne's *Look Back in Anger* in 1956, prose drama has predominated.

In the number of performances given of each of Nicholson's plays, a curve may be traced whose steady fall is in part attributable to the decline of interest in verse drama as a medium. Against at least twenty-four separate presentations of *The Old Man of the Mountains* can be set no more than four of *Birth by Drowning*. This decrease must also, however, be accounted for by a gradual slackening of intensity perceptible in the plays themselves. Though Nicholson considered that *Prophesy to the Wind* and *A Match for the Devil* were technical improvements on *The Old Man of the Mountains,* this first play, for all its frequent echoes of T. S. Eliot and its air of earnest didacticism, remains emotionally his most powerful. It has been performed as recently as 1960. Nicholson once spoke of having for it "a doting father's affection,"[68] which sounds needlessly patronizing: the sense which the play communicates of its author's strongly felt concern for his theme makes its occasional stiffness of technique a minor matter.

Nicholson's own view of his plays is a very modest one: "I make [no] exorbitant claims for the plays. They are only a very minor contribution to modern verse drama, and only to a special and smaller corner in it. But I do feel that they fulfil a purpose, that they can speak to the audiences for which they were designed, and that, in their little way, they give a kind of tang or tone which can be found nowhere else in modern drama."[69]

In that the staging of any play involves a financial risk which demands that the tastes of an audience be taken into account, the mere fact that many acting groups have decided to present Nicholson's plays argues their ability to please their particular audiences. The printing of Nicholson's plays, however, lays them open to the judgment of a less calculable public, which may include readers unlikely to belong to the type of audience to whom they appeal on the stage. Some of these readers may find Nicholson's characteristic habit of drawing his material from the Old Testament merely quaint, and their response to his use of this material limited by memories of bored afternoons in Sunday School. Moving in a half-world neither completely contemporary nor solidly historical, his prophets and his country folk may seem less immediately relevant than the modern urban characters presented by Anne Ridler in her play *The Shadow Factory,* less intellectually interesting than Becket in Eliot's *Murder in the Cathedral,* and less flattering to the connoisseur of sophisticated spiritual problems than St. Anthony in Ronald Duncan's play *This Way to the Tomb.*

The unique "tang" of Nicholson's plays most obviously resides in their localizing of Old Testament themes and characters in his own geographical area and in their use of a poetic language which involves specifically local description and gains energy from an admixture of dialect words and inflections. In using this same method in his poetry—in writing, that is, about what is closest to his own experience—Nicholson manages to communicate without undue restriction of his audience; for he is able to measure precisely the amount of local material he can use without endangering the poem's wider application. He is able to attain a more than provincial appeal because he himself—and it is his own views which his poems express—is more than simply a provincial. In his plays, Nicholson's touch has been less sure: by choosing to depict his biblical figures as ordinary provincial characters—perhaps the only choice open to him, given the kind of people among whom he has spent his life—and by allowing those characters to function on a realistic local level, Nicholson is less able to transcend provinciality. His plays possess vitality and verbal attractiveness, but they allow smaller scope for his mental and imaginative powers than does his poetry. By writing for a certain kind of audience, Nicholson has opted for a necessarily restricted kind of success.

CHAPTER 6

Towards a Conclusion

I *Nicholson and Contemporaries*

IN 1959, the poet-critic George MacBeth published an article in which he postulated the division of twentieth-century British poetry into two kinds: the "conservative tradition" and the "modern movement." The "modern movement" involved "obscurity" and a "constant striving after originality of style," and in it MacBeth grouped such poets as Eliot, Auden, Empson, and Dylan Thomas. The "conservative tradition" was characterized by a striving for clarity and by "a preoccupation with a certain kind of society and the moral role which poetry should play in that society."[1] Despite Nicholson's far from limited awareness of these poets, which, in his earlier work, was reflected in the influence of Eliot and Auden, it seems more accurate to place him in the "conservative tradition": his mature poetry has always eschewed obscurity and has shown, notwithstanding its local context, a concern for general human experience appropriate to a man who once said that "the time has come when the poet needs to forget what differentiates him from other men and to remember what binds him to them."[2]

It was MacBeth's view that, for the greater part of the twentieth century, the "conservative tradition" had been mainly upheld by regional poets; and, though MacBeth did not mention Nicholson, his threefold definition of the regional poet serves as a convenient description of Nicholson's own characteristics:

(1) he often writes about a particular landscape and a particular group of people inhabiting it;
(2) his work avoids technical experiment for its own sake and aims at a conversational directness in words and rhythm;
(3) and he draws on incidents from his daily life to back up moral judgments and psychological insights.[3]

The regional poet whom MacBeth put forward as an example was the Welshman R. S. Thomas, whose work first appeared in England in 1954 in his volume *Song at the Year's Turning.* On the face of it, it would therefore seem possible to compare the poetry of Nicholson and R. S. Thomas. The poetry in *Song at the Year's Turning* was mostly written while Thomas was rector of the hill-farming parish of Manafon in central Wales; and, like Nicholson, Thomas has been concerned with understanding the ways of those among whom he has lived and with making them understandable to people elsewhere. A remark at the end of Thomas's "A Priest to his People," however, indicates a very significant difference between the slant of his work and that of Nicholson:

> You will continue to unwind your days
> In a crude tapestry under the jealous heavens
> To affront, bewilder, yet compel my gaze.

Nicholson's "gaze" at life in Millom and Cumberland has been similarly "compelled," but no trace of "affront" or bewilderment appears in his work.

To define fully Nicholson's kind of regional poetry, one nees to add one more clause to MacBeth's list, one which Nicholson has supplied himself in his article "On Being a Provincial" (1954): "By a provincial I do not mean someone who merely happens to live in the provinces—I mean someone who lives in the place where he was born; the place where his parents live, and his friends and relatives. Someone who has shared from childhood the culture of his native region—the way of life, the pattern of activities."

Though a Welshman who has remained in Wales, R. S. Thomas is by no means the sort of "provincial" Nicholson describes here. Behind the local themes which create in many of Thomas's poems a superficial likeness to those of Nicholson lies a very different kind of personality, one more melancholy, more questioning, and more bitter. Thomas, in his search for a sense of identity with an area and its people, has had many obstacles to overcome—obstacles created by a formal education far more thoroughgoing than Nicholson's, by the unavoidable separateness involved in his clerical status, and by the fact that he is not, apart from his shared Welshness, one by birth with the local communities to which he has ministered.

Indeed, seemingly only one other contemporary British poet comes near to fitting the description of the "provincial" which Nicholson puts forward—the Cornish poet Jack Clemo, who was born in 1916 "in a hamlet seven miles north-west of St. Austell, lodged deep in the gut of the Cornish china-clay industry."[4] Like Nicholson, Clemo has never moved from the place (the house, even) in which he was born; and he has used in his work the imagery of clay and clay pits supplied by his environment. But again, despite superficial similarities, the two poets differ greatly. Clemo, temporarily blind in childhood, and permanently blind since 1955, is a poet much less responsive to his physical surroundings than Nicholson; and the fact that he has also been deaf since the age of eighteen has made his poetry evolve a peculiar, and often eccentric, rhythm and idiom rather than modify, as Nicholson's has done, the rhythms inherent in colloquial speech. Blindness and deafness have both prevented Clemo from sharing in "the culture of his native region," as Nicholson has been able to do: and Clemo uses local imagery not for any intrinsic interest it may possess but almost entirely to express his religious preoccupations. In a word, his poetry is introverted rather than extrovert; and his difference from Nicholson is captured in his statement that "of no man could it be said with less truth that he knows every nook and cranny of his own district."[5]

In "The Black Guillemot" (1967), Nicholson characterized the bird by a phrase which, if the poem is taken as an allegory for the relationship between the writer and his community, seems to be a self-portrait. He said that there was "Not a bird of his kind/ Nesting to the south of him in England." Though Nicholson may, as a regionalist, be bracketed for convenience with R. S. Thomas and Jack Clemo and, in America, with such poets of deeply rooted local allegiance as Robert Frost and John Crowe Ransom, he is in fact, in England at least, a unique figure—unique not just because of his Cumbrian subject matter and imagery but also because of the particularly close identification with his material which he has achieved by spending his whole life in one place.

In this respect, he resembles William Cowper, on whom he published in 1951 a critical study whose perceptiveness is due to "a special intuitive sympathy."[6] Nicholson's involvement with his birthplace of Millom is no less close than was Cowper's with his chosen home of Olney; and the overtone of autobiography which Nicholson's study frequently strikes is nowhere stronger than when he quotes four lines of

Cowper's *The Task:* " 'He is a happy man...'[Cowper] says 'Who, doomed to an obscure but tranquil state,/ Is pleas'd with it, and were he free to choose,/ Would make his fate his choice.' "[7] It may certainly be said of Nicholson that his poetry is the process by which he has turned his "fate" of remaining in one particular area into his "choice" of interpreting that area in such a way that, while still retaining its local identity, it transcends itself and becomes a stage on which universal truths are acted.

To say that a poet is unique is not, of course, to imply that he is a major figure. Nicholson himself makes no extravagant claims for his work: "the provinces" can "remind us of that which is timeless," but "I do not pretend that it is from this sort of provincial background that we shall get our major works of art."[8] Nevertheless, Nicholson is a poet of real importance. His work possesses three prerequisites of poetry: technical skill, imaginative persuasiveness, and the sheer ability of its language to grip the reader's attention. Despite Nicholson's occasional early echoes of other poets—Eliot, Auden, Kathleen Raine—his mature style is very much his own; and in his best poems a handling of rhythm at once vigorous and sensitive combines with a vivid, pungent, and original imagery to produce lines which imprint themselves firmly on the memory. The presence of these qualities—belonging to poetry, pure and simple—makes it worthwhile to try to establish the uniqueness of his position as a poet whose work can be also defined as regional in origin.

II *Reputation and Value*

To present and discuss Nicholson's poetry in such a way as to suggest the value of its contribution to contemporary British poetry has been the purpose of this book. To indicate just where Nicholson stands in the hierarchy of that poetry is a difficult task, for there exists something of a disparity between what seems to be his importance and his critical reputation. Broadcasting in 1963, Nicholson referred in passing to "twenty-five years of being almost totally ignored as a poet."[9] At first sight, this statement is very hard to explain. His poetry, in volume form, has been published by Faber and Faber, which means in the first instance that it measured up to the high standards of T. S. Eliot, Faber's poetry reader; it thus figures in a list which amounts to a roll-call of major twentieth-century reputations. Similarly, the publications in which Nicholson's individual poems have appeared comprise a catalogue of the most influential and prestigious literary magazines of the last thirty years: in England, *Penguin New Writing, Orpheus, Horizon, The Listener, Spectator, New Statesman, The Times Literary Supplement, The London Magazine;* in Italy, *Botteghe Oscure;* and in the United States, *Poetry* (Chicago), *The Southern Review, Harper's, Saturday Review,* and the *New Yorker.* His volumes have never lacked reviews in the most important periodicals, and the majority of these reviews have been favorable.

When a closer look is taken, however, the meaning of Nicholson's statement becomes clearer. For all the eminence of his literary publication, Nicholson has never quite consolidated the kind of reputation which an observer would expect. The singling-out by George MacBeth, in the article already mentioned, of R. S. Thomas as "the only important example" of a regional poet between 1922 and 1955, and the total absence, even, of any reference to Nicholson, are evidence enough of this fact. A number of external reasons suggest themselves. First, the Christian attitudes which probably aided Nicholson's acceptability in the 1940's came to be at a discount in the following decade. Second, he seems to be one of those unfortunate poets who, because they first came to prominence in the 1940s, were indiscriminately discarded by the critic-poets of the 1950s who were reacting against so-called "neo-Romanticism"; it is regrettable, in this connection, that for many years Nicholson was represented in Kenneth Allott's widely known *Penguin Book of Contemporary Verse* (1950) by "Poem for Epiphany," which Allott later admitted to be an atypical choice.[10] And, third, in so far as British literary reputations are made in London, it seems likely that Nicholson's position as a regional poet has put him at a disadvantage.

Nicholson's regional material has been discussed throughout this book simply because, without doing so, the nature of his poetry could not have been made clear. But regionalism is an ingredient of the poetry, not a disadvantage under which it labors; it is a descriptive term, not a limiting concept. With a number of reviewers, the term "regional" has, however, been used as a label, either dismissively, or in such a way that it has ended up by obscuring the poetry which it should merely have described. Whereas Paul Dehn, for instance, felt that Nicholson's poems had a more than regional appeal,[11] an anonymous reviewer in *The Times Literary Supplement* thought that "what is most lacking [in *Rock Face]* is a sense of life going on outside."[12] And whereas a later reviewer in the same periodical praised Nicholson for being "a poet who is at home in the world in which he finds himself," one who "has been wise to school his eye to such minute observation and his lively powers of observation to such faithfulness,"[13] G. S. Fraser accused him of being "a good poet who has become the victim of his formulas. . .Mr. Nicholson's universe. . .seems not various enough."[14]

Admittedly, Nicholson rarely goes outside his own Northern region for his material, but this fact need not be thought to limit the wider application which he gives to it. Nicholson is certainly not the only poet to remain loyal (to rewrite Fraser in less tendentious terms) to a certain kind of subject matter and to a particular tone of voice: the better-known name of Philip Larkin comes to mind here. Alan Ross summed up Nicholson's poetic habits more favorably, and with a more open mind, when he wrote in 1951 that "Nicholson, probably wisely, has decided to work a narrow seam very deeply rather than extend his range more shallowly."[15] There may be suspected behind Fraser's criticism the partial influence of a sort of literary orthodoxy which forms part of the general metropolitan sense of superiority against which Nicholson's article "On Being a Provincial" (1954) was aimed. In the context of this orthodoxy, Nicholson's particular formula—a natural tendency, given his provincial experience, to be most strongly and frequently stimulated by that experience—seems to the London literary critic unfamiliar and unfashionable. A recent anatomist of the North of England, Graham Turner, quoted two North-Country novelists in illustration of the peculiar attitude towards the North of England sometimes found in the South: "novelists like Stan Barstow and Sid Chaplin. . .told me how much they resented constantly being asked *why* they chose to live in the North, as if they were displaying some deplorable eccentricity."[16]

Nicholson himself does not feel that his regional experience is a limitation; it is, for him, the experience of "that which is common to the lives of all of us," and it allows him to feel a sense of community with writers abroad: "When I read those European writers who, in their own countries, might be called provincial—say, Ignazio Silone, telling of peasants in the Italian hills, or François Mauriac of wealthy landowners in the forests behind Bordeaux—then, often, I feel that they are describing a habit and mode of existence that is familiar to me."[17] It is

[159]

heartening to find that this understanding is not in one direction only; for one of the few critics to deal with Nicholson's poetry at any length has been an Italian, Giorgio Melchiori, who devoted a long article to it in 1955. Professor Melchiori took full account of Nicholson's regional background, but he had no difficulty in seeing through it to his "natura genuinamente poetica"[18] and in discovering an affinity between his work and that of the Italian poet Eugenio Montale. Melchiori implicitly suggests that Nicholson's relevance is limited neither to his own region nor to his own country.

Nicholson once commented that "I probably enjoy life far too much to be a good poet."[19] That enjoyment of life is a disqualification for the writing of good poetry is debatable, but enjoyment is certainly a quality apparent in most of Nicholson's work, whether it evinces itself in detailed description of the physical world, in vivid images often verging on conceits, in a general exuberance of rhythm and language, or in a religious optimism which derives ultimately from the "second chance" which Nicholson was given in 1932 when he survived tuberculosis. That ill-health which deprived him of an anticipated university education offered the compensation, unusual for a twentieth-century poet, of rootedness in a half-rural, half-industrial environment in which he could observe more clearly "that which is enduring in life and society."[20]

However nebulous Nicholson's critical reputation may be, his poetry has a strong appeal for another, less vocal audience: an audience, not small, of fellow-provincials in many places, the nature of whose lives would give them an instinctive understanding of the kind of material his poems interpret: "The material which [the provincial artist] uses, the basic imagery and background of his work, is such that [his fellow townsfolk] would recognise, such that in their own way they would find exciting and significant and relevant to their lives. The subjects which he describes, the scenes, the symbols which appear in his work, have all gone in and out of the minds of his fellows like air in and out of their lungs, taking a new meaning from their thoughts, taking a new vitality from their energies."[21]

Nicholson's poetry exemplifies the reciprocity described in this passage—an interdependence of writer and audience; and it is most of all because it does so that Nicholson may reasonably be described as unique among present-day British poets. But unique though he may be as a poet, and in a way which makes him unfamiliar to critics,

Nicholson is by no means unique as a man, especially if his view is borne in mind that "the vast majority of mankind is provincial."[22] Only his poetic talent sets him apart from his fellows; the content of his poetry links him firmly with them. Because his poetry expresses the "timeless," rather than the "changing," elements of natural and human life, Nicholson's work is capable of reaching a wider audience than most modern poets have the opportunity to address. If more critics were willing to admit to themselves their own basic likeness to their fellows, Nicholson's audience could become as wide as he deserves.

Notes and References

Chapter One

1. *Dictionary of World Literary Terms,* ed. J. T. Shipley (London, 1955).

2. Phyllis Bentley, *The English Provincial Novel* (P.E.N. Books) (London, 1941).

3. "The Provincial Tradition," *Times Literary Supplement,* August 15, 1958, p. xix.

4. It is significant, in view of Nicholson's intimate involvement with his region, that in the 1930s his favorite novelist was William Faulkner.

5. Thinly disguised as "Odborough" (which clearly resembles Hodbarrow), Millom is also the setting of Nicholson's two novels, *The Fire of the Lord* (1944) and *The Green Shore* (1947).

6. *Portrait of the Lakes* (London, 1963), p. 66.

7. "Old Main Street, Holborn Hill, Millom," *The Pot Geranium,* London, Faber and Faber, 1954, p. 14.

8. "From Walney Island," *The Pot Geranium,* p. 18.

9. *Provincial Pleasures* (London, 1959), p. 144.

10. Alan Harris, "Millom: A Victorian New Town," *Transactions of the Cumberland and Westmorland Antiquarian and Archaeological Society,* LXVI, New Series (Kendal, 1966), 449-67. I am greatly indebted to the information in this fascinating article.

11. "Bond Street," *The London Magazine,* V, 12 (December, 1958), 47.

12. "A Street in Cumberland," *Rock Face* (London, 1948), p. 13.

13. "Millom Old Quarry," *The Pot Geranium* (1954), p. 11.

14. "Hodbarrow Hollow," *Manchester Guardian,* May 21, 1959.

15. "The Wheel of Fire," *The Listener,* April 17, 1952, p. 630.

16. "The Town Band," *Time and Tide,* March 12, 1955, p. 323.

17. "On Being a Provincial," *The Listener,* August 12, 1954, p. 248.

18. The influence of both denominations is apparent in Nicholson's two novels. *The Fire of the Lord* uses dates in the Anglican ecclesiastical year instead of chapter divisions and one of its main characters, Elsie Holliwell, is a devout Anglican. By contrast, Anthony Pengwilly, the main character in *The Green Shore,* is converted by a

traveling Methodist missioner, and most of the characters attend the Bible Christian chapel.

19. Quoted by Samuel Davis, "Portrait of a Contemporary Poet," *The Methodist Recorder,* April 4, 1957.

20. "The Second Chance," *The Listener,* September 5, 1963, p. 344.

21. Nicholson, Contribution to *They Became Christians,* ed. Dewi Morgan (London, 1966), pp. 99-100.

22. *Ibid.*

23. Letter from Nicholson to George Every, May 3, 1938.

24. *Provincial Pleasures* (1959), pp. 186-87.

25. *They Became Christians,* p. 100.

26. *Portrait of the Lakes* (1963), p. 174.

27. *They Became Christians,* p. 101.

28. "Words and Imagery," in *T. S. Eliot: A Symposium compiled by Tambimuttu and Richard March* (1948). Third Impression (London, 1965), p. 231.

29. "Words and Imagery," p. 234.

30. "The Second Chance" (1963), p. 344.

31. *They Became Christians,* p. 106.

32. A fourth friendship, of strong private importance, was with Enrica Garnier, the daughter of missionary parents. Nicholson first met her in 1936, and the friendship lasted until well into the 1940s. *Five Rivers* is dedicated to her, and the poem "September in Shropshire" records a visit Nicholson paid when the school where she taught was evacuated during the war.

33. Letter from T. S. Eliot to George Every, September 27, 1937.

34. Letter from Nicholson to George Every, September 1, 1937.

35. *Ibid.*

36. *Ibid.,* March 20, 1940.

37. *Ibid.,* May 3, 1938.

38. *They Became Christians,* p. 107.

39. *Ibid.*

40. *They Became Christians,* p. 108.

41. *Ibid.,* p. 107.

42. The poem is unpublished. The capitals in line one are Nicholson's.

Chapter Two

1. This description is found more accessibly in the later guidebook *Portrait of the Lakes* (1963), p. 63.

2. Letter from Nicholson to Bessie Satterthwaite, June 3, 1942.

3. W. H. Auden, *The Orators* (London, 1932), p. 12.

4. Letter from Nicholson to George Every, September 29, 1937.

5. *Ibid.*, September 1, 1937.

6. *Ibid.*, September 29, 1937.

7. *Ibid.*, September 15, 1937.

8. Cf. W. H. Auden and Christopher Isherwood, *The Dog Beneath the Skin* (London, 1935), pp. 15-16.

9. Cf. W. H. Auden, *Collected Shorter Poems 1930-1944* (London, 1950), pp. 31, 36, 94-95.

10. "The Image in My Poetry," *Orpheus,* II (London, 1949), 121.

11. Letter from Nicholson to George Every, February 24, 1938.

12. *Ibid.*, March 20, 1940.

13. See Nicholson, "A Note on Allegory," *Focus One* (London, 1945), pp. 41-42.

14. Nicholson himself testified to this Kafka influence (letter to the writer, May 12, 1968). A chapter on Kafka is included in *Man and Literature* (London, 1943).

15. W. H. Auden, *Collected Shorter Poems,* pp. 58-59.

16. Auden, *op. cit.,* p. 253.

17. When Mrs. C. B. Schiff (the former Bessie Satterthwaite) sent the present writer a copy of "No Man's Land," it was accompanied by a photograph of Swinside stone circle, endorsed on the back "See No Man's Land."

18. See M. J. Tambimuttu (ed.), *Poetry in Wartime* (London, 1942), p. 146.

19. Spender, review in *New Statesman,* April 17, 1943.

20. See, for instance, Reginald Snell, "The Poetry of Norman Nicholson," *The New English Weekly,* August 31, 1944, pp. 151-52.

21. Nicholson seems to have been dissatisfied with the image, as in the version of the poem printed in *Selected Poems* (London, 1966) he suppressed lines 19-20. Unfortunately, his consequent need not to upset the stanza pattern led him also to excise lines 21-22, with the result that the poem's conclusion is now too hurried.

22. Interview with Peter Orr, April 3, 1964. Published in Peter Orr (ed.), *The Poet Speaks* (London, 1966), p. 156.

Chapter Three

1. They are "Corregidor," "Before I was Born," "Love was there in Eden," and "Carol for Holy Innocents' Day."

2. Out of forty poems, twenty are from *The Pot Geranium,* as against eleven from *Rock Face,* and nine from *Five Rivers.*

3. "The Image in my Poetry", *Orpheus,* II (1949), 122.

4. Already used by Wordsworth in "The Horn of Egremont Castle."

5. Letter from Nicholson to the writer, March 8, 1957.

6. Ms. of leading article for *The Times Literary Supplement* on Roger Lloyd's *The Borderland* (London, 1960).

7. *Provincial Pleasures*, p. 184.

8. Elizabeth Jennings, *Christianity and Poetry* (London, 1965), p. 92.

9. T. S. Eliot, *After Strange Gods* (London, 1934), p. 38.

10. "Tell It Out Among the Heathen", *Christian News-Letter*, October, 1956, p. 35.

11. "The Comic Prophet," *The Listener*, August 6, 1953.

12. "Tell It Out Among the Heathen" (1956), p. 37.

13. See "The Comic Prophet" (1953).

14. A. I. Doyle, review of *Five Rivers*, *Scrutiny*, September, 1945.

15. Anonymous review of *Five Rivers*, *The Listener*, October 12, 1944.

16. Expressed in a letter from T. S. Eliot to Anne Ridler, June 17, 1943.

17. Anonymous review in *The Listener*, July 22, 1943.

18. "Millom Delivered," *The Listener*, January 24, 1952, p. 139.

19. "Tell It Out Among the Heathen" (1956), p. 34.

20. John Betjeman, *Daily Herald*, July 6, 1944.

21. Julian Symons, *Tribune*, October 6, 1944.

22. See reviews in *The Times Literary Supplement*, May 8, 1948, and *The Listener*, September 9, 1948.

23. Howard Sergeant, review in *Poetry Quarterly* (date unknown), p. 105.

24. See *The Lakers* (London, 1955), p. 53.

25. "Millom Delivered" (1952), p. 139.

26. The word "pears" in the published poem is a misprint.

27. "The Haystack," *Collected Poems of Andrew Young* (London, 1950), p. 24. See also *Andrew Young: Prospect of a Poet* (London, 1957), pp. 61-68, in which Nicholson comments revealingly on "The Haystack."

28. Kathleen Raine, review of *Rock Face*, *New English Review*, January, 1949.

29. Review of *Rock Face*, *The Times Literary Supplement*, May 8, 1948.

30. Giles Romilly, review in *New Statesman*, April 24, 1948, p. 340.

31. "On Being a Provincial" (1954), p. 249.

32. "The Image in my Poetry," p. 122.

33. Anonymous review, *The Times Literary Supplement*, November 5, 1954, p. 702.

34. "The Image in my Poetry," p. 122.

35. Letter from Nicholson to the writer, March 8, 1957.

36. *Cumberland and Westmorland* (London, 1949), p. 31.

37. When first published in *Horizon,* the poem bore the punning subtitle "Diversions on a Ground." According to Nicholson, its musical structure was prompted by one of Bach's Suites for unaccompanied cello.

38. "Millom Delivered" (1952).

39. *Ibid.*

40. Letter from Nicholson to George Every, January 12, 1951.

41. *Ibid.,* May 9, 1951.

42. Interview with Peter Orr, reprinted in *The Poet Speaks,* p. 158.

Chapter Four

1. This sentence, written in 1970, remained true until the autumn of 1972, when Faber and Faber published a fourth volume of poetry by Nicholson entitled *A Local Habitation;* this contains nearly all the "recent poems" mentioned in Chapter 4 and separately listed in the Selected Bibliography.

2. In conversation with the writer in 1967.

3. Letter from Nicholson to the writer, March 8, 1957.

4. See *Portrait of the Lakes* (1963), p. 76; also *The Listener,* July 14, 1960, pp. 49-50.

5. Though the emphasis on these matters is a new one in Nicholson's poetry, he had written about the Millom of the early years of the twentieth century, and used transposed details of his family history, in Part Two, "The Town," of his novel *The Green Shore* (1947).

6. Letter from Nicholson to the writer, March 2, 1959.

7. "Christmas Candles at Odborough," *Church Times,* December 22, 1961, p. 7.

8. See Nicholson, "Hodbarrow Hollow," *Manchester Guardian,* May 21, 1959, p. 9.

9. Letter from Nicholson to the writer, February 4, 1966.

10. The "King Alfred" is a popular variety of daffodil.

11. Letter from Nicholson to the writer, June 18, 1967.

12. The answer, of course, is: "Because it has a tender behind."

13. *Provincial Pleasures* (1959), p. 108.

14. Letter from Nicholson to the writer, June 18, 1967.

15. *Ibid.*

Chapter Five

1. Letter from Nicholson to the writer, February 11, 1965.

2. Nicholson, "Modern Verse Drama and the Folk-Tradition," *Critical Quarterly* (Summer, 1960), p. 167.

3. Letter from Nicholson to George Every, May 3, 1938.

4. Nicholson, "T. S. Eliot. An Obituary Tribute," *Church Times,* January 8, 1965.

5. Letter from Nicholson to George Every, September 7, 1953.

6. "The Abandoned Muse," *Theatre Arts* (New York) (August-September 1948), p. 70.

7. Review in *Church Times,* April 18, 1946.

8. Nicholson's recovery (not expected by his friends) at the sanatorium may also suggest one reason he is able to present miracles in *The Old Man of the Mountains* without feeling the need to explain the.n away.

9. From Nicholson's program note for the performance of the play at the Newcastle People's Theater, July 20-27, 1946.

10. Letter from Nicholson to the writer, February 11, 1965.

11. From Nicholson's program note for the Newcastle performance, 1946.

12. *Ibid.*

13. A gloss of the unusual term "helm wind" is furnished by Nicholson in *Cumberland and Westmorland* (1949), pp. 52-3.

14. In a letter to the writer (February 11, 1965) Nicholson said: "Unlike Eliot, I feel that there is no harm in letting the audience know that the play is in verse."

15. *Ibid.*

16. J. M. Synge, Preface to *The Playboy of the Western World* (Dublin, 1907).

17. Henry Reed, review in *The Listener,* April 11, 1946.

18. Review in *Poetry Review* (April-May, 1946), p. 142.

19. From Nicholson's program note for performance by the Theatre Club, Carlisle, January 26-30, 1956.

20. Quoted by Nicholson, letter to George Every, c. April, 1946.

21. *Ibid.*

22. Quoted by Nicholson, *ibid.*

23. Cf. Shakespeare, *A Midsummer Night's Dream,* III, 2, 208-11.

24. Letter from Nicholson to George Every, July 23, 1951.

25. Gerard Fay, review in *Time and Tide,* August 18, 1951.

26. Peter Forster, review in *Observer,* August 12, 1951.

27. In a letter to George Every (October 7, 1951) Nicholson said that the reaction "was what I had expected."

28. *Ibid.*

29. Letter from Nicholson to George Every, May 9, 1951.

30. *Ibid.,* March 13, 1952. Miss Keily had been a member of the original Pilgrim Players, but had in 1942 been appointed religious drama adviser to the Council of Christian Communities in Sheffield.

31. *Ibid.*

32. *Ibid.*

33. *Ibid.*, February 14, 1953.

34. *Ibid.*

35. "The Comic Prophet," *The Listener,* August 6, 1953.

36. Cf. *A Match for the Devil* (London, 1955), pp. 54-55.

37. Letter from Nicholson to George Every, February 14, 1953.

38. Letter from Pamela Keily to the writer, February 5, 1968.

39. Letter from Nicholson to George Every, February 14, 1953.

40. *Ibid.*

41. T. S. Eliot, *Poetry and Drama* (London, 1951), p. 14.

42. Letter from Nicholson to William Brasmer, September 24, 1953.

43. Much of the background for the play was provided by George Adam Smith, *The Historical Geography of the Holy Land* (London, 1894). For the language of the last three lines of the quotation, cf. 1896 edition (Revised), pp. 382-83.

44. "The Comic Prophet" (1953).

45. This is the only survival in the finished play of an earlier plot which had drawn as much from the First Book of Samuel as from the Book of Hosea.

46. Letter from Nicholson to George Every, August 28, 1953.

47. Letter from Nicholson to the writer, February 11, 1965.

48. Letter from Nicholson to George Every, March 13, 1952.

49. Of the Department of Semitic Languages, University of Manchester.

50. A "lonning" is a lane or back alley.

51. Review, *Manchester Guardian,* September 6, 1955.

52. Letter from Nicholson to George Every, August 21, 1953.

53. Letter from Nicholson to William Brasmer, September 10, 1953.

54. *The Sunday Times,* September 6, 1953.

55. *Church of England Newspaper,* September 4, 1953.

56. Letter from Nicholson to the writer, February 10, 1969.

57. Letter from Nicholson to George Every, September 7, 1953.

58. Letter from Nicholson to William Brasmer, November 5, 1953.

59. Letter from Pamela Keily to the writer, February 5, 1968.

60. Letter from Nicholson to George Every, January 2, 1958.

61. Nicholson's original title, *What the Doctor Ordered,* though understandably vetoed by the play's commissioners, better sums up the "folksy" atmosphere of the play.

62. Review, *Church Times,* June 3, 1960.

63. Review, *The Times Literary Supplement,* July 8, 1960.

64. Letter from Nicholson to George Every, July 20, 1959.

65. Nicholson's geographical knowledge in this play, as in *A Match*

for the Devil, derives from George Adam Smith, *A Historical Geography of the Holy Land.* See especially pp. 119, 122, 327 (Fourth Edition Revised, 1896).

66. Letter from Pamela Keily to the writer, February 5, 1968.

67. "Drama as the Expression of Religion," *Christian News-Letter,* Supplement, No. 208 (May 17, 1944), p. 12.

68. Letter from Nicholson to George Every, July 23, 1951.

69. Letter from Nicholson to the writer, February 11, 1965.

Chapter Six

1. George MacBeth, "Regional Poetry," part of a Symposium on "Poetry since the War," *The London Magazine* (November, 1959).

2. "The Comic Prophet" (1953).

3. MacBeth, *op. cit.*

4. Charles Causley, "The World of Jack Clemo": introduction to Jack Clemo, *The Map of Clay* (London, 1961), p. 7.

5. Jack Clemo, *Confession of a Rebel* (London, 1949), p. 199.

6. Note on dust cover, *William Cowper* (London, 1951).

7. *Ibid.*, p. 99. Cowper, *The Task,* VI, 11. 906 ff.

8. "On Being a Provincial" (1954), p. 248.

9. "The Second Chance" (1963), p. 344.

10. Cf. Kenneth Allott, *Penguin Book of Contemporary Verse* (London, 1962), p. 284.

11. Paul Dehn, in his review of *Rock Face, Time and Tide,* May 1, 1948.

12. Review of *Rock Face, The Times Literary Supplement,* May 8, 1948.

13. Review of *The Pot Geranium, The Times Literary Supplement,* November 5, 1954, p. 702.

14. G. S. Fraser, in his review of *The Pot Geranium, New Statesman,* May 29, 1954.

15. Alan Ross, *Poetry 1945-1950* (London, 1951), p. 33.

16. Graham Turner, *The North Country* (London, 1967), p. 13.

17. "On Being a Provincial" (1954), p. 249.

18. Giorgio Melchiori, "Norman Nicholson e altri poeti inglesi," *Lo Spettatore Italiano* VIII (April, 1955), p. 152.

19. *The Poet Speaks,* Argo Records RG 152.

20. "On Being a Provincial" (1954), p. 249.

21. *Ibid,* p. 248.

22. *Ibid,* p. 248.

Selected Bibliography

Primary Sources
(Listed chronologically and by genre)

1. Volumes of Poetry
Selected Poems (Includes works by J. C. Hall and Keith Douglas.)
    London: John Bale and Staples, 1943.
Five Rivers. London: Faber and Faber, 1944. (Second Impression,
    August, 1944. Third Impression, September, 1945.) New York:
    E. P. Dutton & Co., 1945.
Rock Face. London: Faber and Faber, 1948.
The Pot Geranium. London: Faber and Faber, 1954.
Selected Poems. London: Faber and Faber, 1966.
No Star on the Way Back: Ballads and Carols. Manchester: Manchester
    Institute of Contemporary Arts, 1967.
A Local Habitation. London: Faber and Faber, 1972.

2. Plays
The Old Man of the Mountains. London: Faber and Faber, 1946.
    (Second Impression, 1946. Third Impression Revised, 1950.
    Fourth Impression, 1955.)
Prophesy to the Wind. London: Faber and Faber, 1950.
A Match for the Devil. London: Faber and Faber, 1955.
Birth by Drowning. London: Faber and Faber, 1960.

3. Fiction
"Pisgah" (Short Story). *New English Weekly*, September 15, 1938, pp.
    343-44.
The Fire of the Lord. London: Nicholson and Watson, 1944. New
    York: E. P. Dutton & Co., 1946.
The Green Shore. London: Nicholson and Watson, 1947.

4. Criticism
Man and Literature. London: S.C.M. Press, 1943.

[170]

H. G. Wells. London: Arthur Barker, 1950. Denver: Alan Swallow, 1950.

William Cowper. London: John Lehmann, 1951.

William Cowper. London: Longmans, Green for The British Council, 1960.

5. Broadcast Talks Published
Enjoying It All. London: Waltham Forest Books, 1964.

6. Works Edited
Anthology of Religious Verse. London: Penguin Books, 1942.
Wordsworth: An Introduction and Selection. London: Phoenix House, 1949. Toronto: Dent, 1949.

7. Topography and Miscellaneous
Cumberland and Westmorland. London: Robert Hale, 1949.
The Lakers: The Adventures of the First Tourists. London: Robert Hale, 1955.
Provincial Pleasures. London: Robert Hale, 1959.
Portrait of the Lakes. London: Robert Hale, 1963.
Greater Lakeland. London: Robert Hale, 1969.

8. Uncollected Poems (excluding unpublished poems) to 1970.
"May Day," *The Serpent* (1937).
"Song for 7 p.m.," *Poetry* (Chicago) (March, 1938).
"Behead a God," *Bolero,* No. 2 (Winter, 1938).
"Poem beside a War Memorial," *Bolero,* No. 2 (Winter, 1938).
"Aubade on Bank Holiday," *New English Weekly* (1938).
"Sonnet for an Introvert," *Poetry* (Chicago) (January, 1939).
"Prayer for a Political Meeting," *New English Weekly* (January 12, 1939).
"No Man's Land," *The Southern Review,* V, 2 (1940), 372-74.
"The Burning Tarn," *The Southern Review,* VII, 4 (1942), 867-68.
"Sonnet for Good Friday," *Poetry in Wartime,.* ed. M. J. Tambimuttu. London: Faber and Faber, 1942, p. 74
"Carol for Holy Innocents' Day," *Anthology of Religious Verse,* London: Penguin Books, 1942, p. 89.
"Inscription for a Calendar," *Poetry in Wartime.* London: Faber and Faber, 1942, p. 115.
"Song for St. Gregory of Nyssa," *Today's New Poets,* London: Resurgam Books, 1943.
"Lullaby," *New Statesman,* (September 28, 1946).
"Gravel," *Tribune* (July 22, 1949).

"Lines Addressed to the Wise Men of Borrowdale," *Time and Tide* (November 12, 1949).

"Waking," *British Weekly* (January 18, 1951).

"The Footballer," *New Statesman* (January 27, 1951).

"When that Aprille," *Time and Tide* (April 28, 1951).

"The Poet Rejects an Occasion for a Poem," *The Times Literary Supplement* (December 5, 1952).

"On Suspected Dry Rot in the Roof of a Parish Church," *New Statesman* (July 25, 1953).

"Choral Prelude," *New Statesman* (October 9, 1954).

"The Affirming Blasphemy," *The Times Literary Supplement* (December 10, 1954).

"Peculiar Honours," *Church Times* (December 24, 1954).

"Ferry on the Mersey," *Time and Tide* (1954).

"Under the Auspices of the County Council," *Time and Tide* (1955).

"September on the Mosses," *The London Magazine*, II, 1 (January, 1955), 17.

"Birthday Card," *Time and Tide* (July 2, 1955).

"Old Man at a Cricket Match," *New Statesman* (January 14, 1956).

"Of this Parish," *The Grapevine* (c. 1956), p. 13.

"Windscale," *New Statesman* (November 30, 1957).

"Scree," *Northern Broadsheet No. 4.* Kendal: Titus Wilson, Spring, 1958.

"Bond Street," *The London Magazine*, V, 12 (Dec. 1958), p. 47.

"Christmas Carol for the First Man in the Moon," *House Beautiful* (December, 1959).

"The Seventeenth of the Name," *The Times Literary Supplement* (September 9, 1965), p. 772.

"A Local Preacher's Goodbye," *Stand* VIII, 2 (1966), 5.

"The Elvers," *Stand* VIII, 2 (1966), 4.

"Have You Been to London?" *Poems,* edited for the Poetry Book Society by Eric W. White. London, Christmas, 1966.

"The Riddle," *The Malahat Review*, No. 3 (July, 1967).

"The Cock's Nest," *The Transatlantic Review*, No. 31 (Winter 1968-69), p. 61.

"The Borehole," *The Malahat Review*, No. 9 (January, 1969).

"Great Day," *New Statesman* (February 14, 1969).

"To the Memory of a Millom Musician," *Stand* X, 3 (1969), 6.

"The Black Guillemot," *Stand* X, 3 (1969), 7.

"On the Closing of Millom Ironworks: September 1968," *English,* XVIII, 100 (Spring, 1969), 19.

"Bee Orchid at Hodbarrow," *Stand* XI, 1 (1969-70), 30-31.

9. Selected Articles
"A Note on Allegory," *Focus One* (ed. B. Rajan and Andrew Pearse). London: Dennis Dobson, 1945, pp. 41-42.
"William Faulkner," *The New Spirit* (ed. E. W. Martin). London: Dennis Dobson, 1946, pp. 32-41.
"The Abandoned Muse," *Theatre Arts* (New York). (Aug. - Sept., 1948), p. 70.
"Words and Imagery," in *T. S. Eliot* (A Symposium compiled by M. J. Tambimuttu and Richard March). London., 1948. Third Edition, London: Frank and Cass, 1965, pp. 231-34.
"The Poet Needs an Audience," *Orpheus*, I (c. 1949).
"The Image in My Poetry," *Orpheus*, II (1949), 120-23.
"Notes on the Way" ("The Affirmative Way"), *Time and Tide* (July 21, 1951, p. 697, and July 28, 1951, p. 719).
"The Wheel of Fire," *The Listener* (April 17, 1952), pp. 629-30.
"Notes on the Way," *Time and Tide* (August 9, 1952), pp. 903-04.
"The Comic Prophet," *The Listener* (August 6, 1953).
"Notes on the Way" ("His Own Boss"), *Time and Tide* (July 24, 1954), pp. 987-88.
"On Being a Provincial," *The Listener* (August 12, 1954), pp. 248-49.
"Notes on the Way" ("The Town Band"), *Time and Tide* (March 12, 1955), pp. 323-24.
"Tell It Out Among the Heathen: The Christian Poet Today," *Christian News-Letter* (October, 1956), pp. 33-38.
Contribution (pp. 61-68) to *Andrew Young: Prospect of a Poet* (ed. Leonard Clark). London: Rupert Hart-Davis, 1957.
"Where England Begins," *The Listener* (June 26, 1958), pp. 1051-54.
"The Provincial Tradition," *The Times Literary Supplement* (August 15, 1958), p. xix.
"No Poetry in Railways," *The Listener* (December 4, 1958), pp. 922-24.
"Arnold Bennett," in *English Critical Essays* (ed. Derek Hudson). London: Oxford University Press, 1958.
"Hodbarrow Hollow," *"Manchester Guardian* (May 21, 1959), p. 9.
"Modern Verse Drama and the Folk-Tradition," *Critical Quarterly* (Summer, 1960), pp. 166-70.
"Christmas Candles at Odborough: Childhood Memories Forty Years On," *Church Times* (December 22, 1961), p. 7.
Answer to Questionnaire on Modern Poetry, *The London Magazine* (February, 1962), pp. 52-53.
"The Second Chance," *The Listener* (September 5, 1963), pp. 343-44.
"Crossing the Duddon Sands," *Yorkshire Post* (July 3, 1965).

[173]

NORMAN NICHOLSON

Biographical Introduction to Self-Selection of poems, in *Poets of Our Time* (ed. F. E. S. Finn). London: John Murray, 1965, pp. 117-18.
Interview with Peter Orr (pp. 231-34) in *The Poet Speaks*. London: Routledge and Kegan Paul, 1966, pp. 155-60.
Contribution to *They Became Christians* (ed. Dewi Morgan). London: A. R. Mowbray and Co., 1966, pp. 97-108.
"The Long Poem," *Stand* VIII, 3 (1966-1967), 66-70.

Secondary Sources

ANONYMOUS. "At Home with Norman Nicholson," *Cumbria* (April, 1968), pp. 12-17. Personal close-up of Nicholson in his home and town environment.
DAICHES, DAVID. *The Present Age (After 1920)*. London: The Cresset Press, 1958. Rather superficially brackets Nicholson's first play with the 1945 Mercury Season plays of Anne Ridler and Ronald Duncan. Misleadingly suggests, or appears to suggest (159), that Nicholson imitated "the later Eliot."
FRASER, G. S. *The Modern Writer and His World*. London, Derek Verschoyle, 1953. Penguin Books, 1964. Considers that in Nicholson's plays, and in those of Anne Ridler and Ronald Duncan, "an honorable didactic intention was much more in evidence than a properly dramatic grasp of situation or character." (Penguin, 226).
GARDNER, PHILIP. "The Provincial Poetry of Norman Nicholson," *The University of Toronto Quarterly*, XXXVI, 3, (April, 1967), 274-94. Traces the development of Nicholson's poetry in terms of its changing use of regional material.
"No Man Is an Island: Norman Nicholson's Novels," *A Review of International English Literature*, III, 1 (January, 1972), 44-53. Comments on Nicholson's two novels, *The Fire of the Lord* and *The Green Shore;* points to personal, religious, and regional motifs which they have in common with each other and with Nicholson's poetry.
HAY, DANIEL. "Norman Nicholson," *Library Review* (Spring, 1967), pp. 5-9. Descriptive appreciation of most of Nicholson's books by the Borough Librarian of Whitehaven, Cumberland; feels that Nicholson is "by far the most outstanding writer that Cumberland has produced in the present century."
MELCHIORI, GIORGIO. "Norman Nicholson e altri poeti inglesi," *Lo*

Spettatore Italiano, VIII (April, 1955), 152-57. Discusses Nicholson's themes and techniques very perceptively side-by-side with the work of such contemporaries as George Barker, Vernon Watkins, Laurie Lee, and W. S. Graham. Melchiori feels that Nicholson's poetry, with its "natural concrete images" and its "descriptive lucidity," is more akin to some modern Italian poetry than to that of his English compatriots.

MORGAN, KATHLEEN E. "Some Christian Themes in the Poetry of Norman Nicholson," *A Review of English Literature,* V, 3 (July, 1964), 70-78. Examination, illustrated by quotations from both poems and plays, of Nicholson's vivid use of religious and natural imagery, and of the mutually reinforcing effect of these two elements in his work.
Christian Themes in Contemporary Poets. London: S.C.M. Press, 1965. "The Word in Creation." An expansion of the article above, with a wider range of illustrative examples.

ROSS, ALAN. *Poetry 1945-1950.* London: Longmans, Green, for The British Council, 1951. "Landscapes and Language." Comments favorably on Nicholson's "strict control" of language and feeling to express a "complete absorption" in the material provided by his regional landscape.

SERGEANT, HOWARD. "A Northern Poet: Norman Nicholson," *Northern Review* (August, 1946), pp. 132-37. Attempt to draw attention to the neglected contribution of regional, particularly North-country, poets to their national literature. Praises vividness and vigor of Nicholson's poetry, which derives from a close identification with "his native earth."

STANFORD, DEREK. *The Freedom of Poetry.* London: Falcon Press, 1947. Contains a twenty-page study of Nicholson, in addition to studies of Kathleen Raine, Anne Ridler, Alex Comfort, etc. First serious appraisal of Nicholson; a brief, but both acute and sympathetic, survey of his published work up to 1946.

SKELTON, ROBIN. "The Poems of Norman Nicholson," *Stand,* X, 3, (1969), 8-15. Initially, a salutary view of Nicholson simply as a poet (rather than as a regional poet); marred finally by a perversely over-intellectual emphasis, which makes itself particularly felt in comments on specific quotations.

SPANOS, WILLIAM V. *The Christian Tradition in Modern British Verse Drama: The Poetics of Sacramental Time.* New Brunswick, New Jersey: Rutgers University Press, 1967. Contains a lengthy discussion of *The Old Man of the Mountains* and a sizeable footnote on *A Match for the Devil.* Spanos thinks Nicholson's use of the miraculous likely to be a stumbling block for "the modern secular audience."

WEALES, GERALD. *Religion in Modern English Drama.* Philadelphia: University of Pennsylvania Press, 1961. Very informative on the Pilgrim Players (Ch. VI) and the 1945 Mercury Season (Ch. X).

WILLIAMS, RAYMOND. *Drama from Ibsen to Eliot.* London: Chatto and Windus, 1952. Discusses *The Old Man of the Mountains,* but rather carelessly in part; the influence of T. S. Eliot is shown by particular reference to an Interlude speech by the Raven, which Nicholson had already eliminated in his revised version of the play published in 1950.

Index